MAR 15 2004 Dojre

D1544633

For Reference
Do Not Take
From the Library

# A GUIDE TO

# POPULAR U.S. LANDMARKS

AS LISTED IN

## THE NATIONAL REGISTER OF HISTORIC PLACES

## RICHARD GUY WILSON, PH.D.

DEPARTMENT OF ARCHITECTURAL HISTORY
SCHOOL OF ARCHITECTURE
UNIVERSITY OF VIRGINIA
GENERAL EDITOR

**Franklin Watts**
**A Division of Scholastic Inc.**
New York Toronto London Auckland Sydney Mexico City New Delhi Hong Kong
Danbury, Connecticut

**DEVELOPED, DESIGNED, AND PRODUCED BY**
**BOOK BUILDERS LLC**

BOOK BUILDERS is grateful to the professional historians at the NATIONAL REGISTER OF HISTORIC PLACES for their help in the preparation of this book.

ABOUT THE NATIONAL REGISTER. The National Register of Historic Places is the country's official list of places that have played important roles in American history. If you would like more information about the National Register of Historic Places, log on to the National Register Web site at www.cr.nps.gov/nr/. You also can search the Web site's database, called the National Register Information System (NRIS), by name, city, state, or historic theme. Hundreds of places have been linked together in travel itineraries that are organized geographically or thematically. For teachers, there are also dozens of lesson plans based on historic places.

For *A Guide to Popular U.S. Landmarks*, National Register staff helped identify places with compelling stories, recommended specific places that would be interesting to students and relevant to their school research, and reviewed the text to make sure that the places chosen are listed in the National Register. Except for the United States Capitol, the White House, and the Supreme Court, which are National Historic Landmarks, all of the places included in this book are listed in the National Register of Historic Places.

**Photographs by permission of: Alabama Bureau of Tourism & Travel,** Dan Brothers, photographer: 5; **Arkansas Department of Parks & Tourism:** 11 *right*; **Bettman/CORBIS:** 11 *left*, 101; **Biltmore Estate:** 75; **California Tourism,** Robert Holmes, photographer: 13, 15; **Defense Visual Information Center:** 109; **Delaware Tourism Office:** 20; **Durango & Silverton Narrow Gauge Railroad and Museum:** 17; **Adina Watkins Dyer,** photographer: 35; **Georgia Department of Industry, Trade & Tourism:** 24, 25; **Gettysburg Convention & Visitors Center,** Paul Witt, photographer: 84; **Girls and Boys Town:** 62; **Greenbrier Hotel and Boyd Tamney Cross Marketing:** 111; **Hawaii Visitors & Convention Bureau:** 27; **Jeffery Howe:** 49; **Idaho Travel Council:** 30; **William R. Iseminger:** 31; **JakeMcGuire.com:** 121; **Kentucky School for the Deaf,** Chris Rhoden, photographer, 40; **Library of Congress, Historic American Building Survey:** 8, 37 *right*, 55, 57, 58, 64, 78, 89, cover inset *middle*; **Library of Congress, Historic American Buildings Survey, National Park Service,** drawn by Douglas Pancoast, 1991: 39; **Library of Congress, Historic American Engineering Record:** 61, 71; **Louisiana Office of Tourism:** 42, 44; **Maine Historic Preservation Commission:** 45; **Maryland Office of Tourism,** Tom Darden, photographer, 47; courtesy of **The Mount Washington Hotel & Resort,** 65; ©**Mystic Seaport, CT:** 18; **National Archives and Records Administration (NARA):** 28; **National Park Service:** 33, 69, 115; **New Jersey Department of Environmental Protection, Division of Parks and Forestry,** 69; **NYC & Company, Inc.:** 72; **North Dakota Tourism,** Clayton Wolt, photographer: 77; **Oklahoma Tourism,** Fred M. Marvel, photographer: 80; **Ripon Area Chamber of Commerce:** 113; **Rokeby Museum:** 103; **San Antonio Convention & Visitors Bureau,** Nancy H. Belcher, photographer: 99; **South Dakota Tourism,** Chad Coppess, photographer: 93; **Spindletop Gladys City, Boomtown Museum:** 96; **State Historical Society of Iowa:** 37 *left*; **Tennessee Tourism:** 95; **Timberline Lodge:** 82; **Travel Michigan:** 53; **U.S. Department of the Interior, Bureau of Reclamation:** cover *main image*; **U.S. Navy,** John E. Gay, photographer: 50, cover inset *bottom*; **University of Virginia,** Bill Sublette, photographer: 107, cover inset *top*; **Valley Forge Convention and Visitors Bureau:** 86; **Vassar College,** Megan Casey, photographer: 73; **VISIT FLORIDA:** 22; **Washington, D.C. Convention & Tourism Corporation:** 117, 119; ©**Well-Traveled Images,** David J. Eicher: 91, 105. Design by Jon Glick for Book Builders LLC.

Every effort has been made to obtain permission to use copyrighted material.
The publishers would appreciate errors or omissions being brought to their attention.


Library of Congress Cataloging-in-Publication Data

A guide to popular U.S. landmarks / Richard Guy Wilson, general editor.
        p. cm. — (Watts reference)
    Summary: Highlights major landmarks in each of the fifty states and the nation's capital and lists other important historic sites in each.
    Includes bibliographical references and index.
    ISBN 0-531-12052-X
    1. Historic sites—United States—Juvenile literature. 2. United States—History, Local—Juvenile literature. [1. Historic sites. 2. United States—History, Local.] I. Wilson, Richard Guy, 1940– . II. Series.


E159.G83 2003
973—dc21
                                                                    2002038004

©2003 Franklin Watts
A Division of Scholastic Inc.
All rights reserved. Published simultaneously in Canada.
Printed in the United States of America.
1  2  3  4  5  6  7  8  9  10   R  12  11  10  09  08  07  06  05  04  03

# CONTENTS

**NOTE TO THE READER**
iii

**HOW TO USE THIS BOOK/NOTE TO THE EDUCATOR**
iv

**LANDMARKS BY STATE, ALABAMA TO WYOMING AND WASHINGTON, D.C.**
5

**SITES-AT-A-GLANCE**
123

**SELECTED BIBLIOGRAPHY**
125

**INDEX**
126

## NOTE TO THE READER

History is made in many ways—by people, events, and places. Places where something special happened are frequently called landmarks. They commemorate where a person protested segregation, where a military battle was fought, where a famous person lived, or where a breakthrough in knowledge occurred.

Landmarks can also be important buildings, such as a state capitol, a house known for its beauty, or a temple known for its architecture. A place of business might be a landmark, as might a church, a mill, or even a park that people have admired for its landscaping.

What makes a landmark is varied, as this book shows. *A Guide to Popular U.S. Landmarks* is an invitation to explore the wonderful world of historic sites and landmarks.

There are more than 75,000 places listed in the National Register of Historic Places, America's official list of important places, and more than 2,300 of them are listed as National Historic Landmarks. More are added to both lists all the time. The more than 200 you will find here might help you think about what is important in your town as well as what already has, or should, make history.

—Richard Guy Wilson, *General Editor*

# HOW TO USE THIS BOOK

The entries in *A Guide to Popular U.S. Landmarks* are arranged in alphabetical order, by state, from Alabama to Wyoming, followed by the nation's capital, Washington, D.C. Each entry not only highlights key landmarks in each of the 50 states but also names other important historic sites.

Many entries in the guide contain cross-references. These are words or phrases in SMALL CAPITAL LETTERS that point you to related subjects discussed elsewhere in the book. Whenever you see a cross-reference at the end of a state's entry, you can find more information under another state.

Scattered throughout the guide are special features, which appear in lightly colored boxes. "Profile" boxes highlight people who were important to the story behind a landmark. City boxes focus on key facts about the city or place where the landmark is located.

The index at the back of the book will help you to locate people, places, and topics quickly. You also will find a list of books and Web sites where you can research more information on the nation's historic landmarks.

—Darrell J. Kozlowski, *Editor*

# NOTE TO THE EDUCATOR

This guide gathers in one place a compelling variety of the more than 2,300 places that are listed by the secretary of the interior as National Historic Landmarks. The guide can be used in conjunction with local and national history classes to encourage a sense of place. Through a sampling of sites, young readers will become aware of the manifold dimensions to United States history. We have sought to include a wide range of landmarks that concern both individuals and groups, that are known for their beauty or their architecture, or that commemorate historic events.

How does a place become a National Historic Landmark? The official Landmarks Program was established in 1960 to recognize and preserve unique places that capture the nation's heritage and link past generations to future generations. National Park Service personnel, with outside help from individuals and state and local governments, draw up nominations, and an advisory board makes formal recommendations to the secretary of the interior. The list is constantly expanding and evolving.

We hope that this book will help young readers expand their idea of history as they research the meaning behind places. It also will help illustrate the dynamic interaction between the physical, manufactured world and the natural world.

—Richard Guy Wilson, *General Editor*

# ALABAMA

## MONTGOMERY

**DEXTER AVENUE KING MEMORIAL BAPTIST CHURCH** Located one block from the Alabama State Capitol, the first church where civil rights leader Martin Luther King, Jr., served as pastor and the original headquarters of a historic boycott against segregated city buses in 1955 and 1956.

In the mid-1950s, the Reverend Dr. Martin Luther King, Jr., began preaching in the Dexter Avenue Baptist Church, built in 1878.

**HISTORY** Originally called the Second Colored Baptist Church of Montgomery, the small brick-and-wood structure was completed in 1878. It was founded by members of another Baptist church in Montgomery who broke away to form their own congregation.

Later renamed the Dexter Avenue Baptist Church, it became a center of the early civil rights movement in the mid-1950s. Martin Luther King, Jr., a powerful speaker, was named pastor in September 1954. In December 1955, Rosa Parks, a seamstress who lived in the Cleveland Avenue apartments, was arrested for refusing to give up her seat in the "whites-only" section of a city bus. Leaders of the African American community met at the Dexter Avenue Baptist Church and organized a boycott of the bus system. They created the Montgomery Improvement Association to spearhead the boycott, and they named King as its president.

### ❖ MONTGOMERY ❖

- First settled by the French in 1817
- Located in east central Alabama
- State capital of Alabama, which is bordered by Georgia, Florida, Mississippi, and Tennessee
- Called the "Cradle of the Confederacy" because the government of the Confederate States of America was founded there in February 1861 and the city served as its first capital.

A prominent civil rights leader and winner of the 1964 Nobel Peace Prize, Dr. King was a Baptist minister. His campaign of nonviolent protest helped achieve progress in the struggle for racial equality in America. He rose to prominence as an organizer of the 1955–1956 Bus Boycott in Montgomery, Alabama. In 1957, he became the first president of the Southern Christian Leadership Conference, a leading civil rights group. On August 28, 1963, King delivered his famous "I Have a Dream" speech at a massive rally in WASHINGTON, D.C. He was assassinated in Memphis, TENNESSEE, on April 4, 1968.

For nearly a year, Montgomery buses were virtually empty as African American boycotters walked or carpooled to their destinations. Organizers and volunteers met regularly at the church to coordinate the effort. Finally, in November 1956, the United States Supreme Court ruled that Alabama's bus segregation laws were unconstitutional. By law, the Montgomery bus company had to allow blacks to sit together with whites.

The Montgomery Bus Boycott became a model for grassroots resistance in the fight against racial segregation. Martin Luther King, Jr., was propelled into a position of leadership in the civil rights movement.

TODAY The Dexter Avenue Baptist Church, located at 454 Dexter Avenue, is now open to the public. Visitors can see the sanctuary where King preached. A large mural depicts events in his life and the modern civil rights movement. Designated a National Historic Landmark in 1974.

## TUSCUMBIA

IVY GREEN The birthplace of Helen Keller (1880–1968), humanitarian, author, and pioneer in education for the deaf, blind, and disabled. The 10-acre (4.04-hectare) property, located in northwestern Alabama, includes the cottage in which Keller was born and the house in which she spent her early childhood. Also on the grounds is the water pump where the seven-year-old Keller had her communication breakthrough—associating the manual alpha-

### ❖ TUSCUMBIA ❖

- First settled by Europeans about 1820
- Located in the northwestern corner of Alabama, one of the state's Quad Cities (with Florence, Muscle Shoals, and Sheffield)
- Site of Belle Mont, one of the state's first great plantation houses; and of the Alabama Music Hall of Fame

bet with letters and words—with teacher Anne Sullivan. Ivy Green was built in 1820. Today, it houses a museum dedicated to the life and work of Helen Keller. Designated a National Historic Landmark in 1992.

---

## MORE SITES

**FORT MORGAN** Confederate fortress at the entrance of Mobile Bay, site of an important Civil War battle in August 1864. A Union naval force led by Admiral David Farragut sailed past underwater mines and enemy fire to seal off the Confederacy's last major Gulf Coast port. At a critical moment, Farragut shouted the famous words, "Damn the torpedoes, full speed ahead!" Designated a National Historic Landmark in 1960.

**TUSKEGEE INSTITUTE** A trade school for African Americans founded in 1881 by Booker T. Washington (1856–1915). Among its faculty was Dr. George Washington Carver, whose research revolutionized Southern agriculture and led to new consumer uses for the peanut, the sweet potato, and the pecan. The school is also well known as the training center of the Tuskegee airmen, African American fighter pilots who fought during World War II. Today, Tuskegee University is one of the nation's foremost centers of higher learning for African Americans. Designated a National Historic Landmark in 1965.

# ALASKA

## NOME

**ANVIL CREEK GOLD DISCOVERY SITE** Located just east of the town of Nome on the Bering Sea, the site of the first major gold strike on mainland Alaska on September 20, 1898. The discovery of gold deposits in Anvil Creek by three Scandinavians—Jafet Lindeberg, Erik Lindblom, and John Brynteson—touched off a stampede of gold seekers. More than 12,000 miners and prospectors arrived in the area by 1900. Most of them lived in a rowdy tent-and-cabin settlement along the oceanfront. Lawlessness was common in the town. By 1910, the gold fields around Nome had yielded more than $57 million. Designated a National Historic Landmark in 1965.

### ❖ NOME ❖

- City founded in 1898 when gold was discovered
- Located in western Alaska, which is bordered by the Canadian provinces of Yukon and British Columbia, the Pacific Ocean, the Bering Sea, and the Arctic Ocean
- A port accessible by ship, but only during the summer
- The population of Nome and its surrounding area is chiefly Native Alaskan. Native handicrafts and gold mining are the mainstays of the local economy.

**ST. MICHAEL'S CATHEDRAL** A Russian Orthodox church in Sitka and the foremost nineteenth-century landmark of Russian culture in North America. Built between 1844 and 1848, it served until 1872 as the Seat of the Russian Orthodox Diocese that governed North America. Thereafter, it served as the Seat of the Diocese of Alaska. An outstanding example of Russian church architecture, the original onion-domed structure was destroyed by a fire in 1966. The present building is an authentic reconstruction that still stands out on the Sitka skyline. Priceless religious icons and other artifacts are on display inside. Designated a National Historic Landmark in 1962.

Using plans drawn up by the Historic American Buildings Survey, St. Michael's Cathedral was authentically rebuilt after a 1966 fire.

❖ **SITKA** ❖

- First settled by Russians in 1799
- Located in southeastern Alaska on Baranof Island in the Alexander Archipelago
- Served as the capital of Russian America until 1867 and the capital of the Alaska Territory until 1900

MORE SITES

**AMERICAN FLAG-RAISING SITE** Location in Sitka where the Russian flag was lowered and the American flag was raised upon the formal transfer of Alaska to the United States on September 18, 1867. The United States had paid Russia $7.2 million for 589,757 square miles (1,527,470 square kilometers) of Alaskan land. No buildings remain on the site, but it is rich in historical archaeological artifacts. Designated a National Historic Landmark in 1962.

# ARIZONA

## GRAND CANYON NATIONAL PARK

**GRAND CANYON VILLAGE** Located on the South Rim of the Grand Canyon, the largest tourist center for Grand Canyon National Park. Perched nearly 1 mile (1.6 kilometers) above the base of the gorge, the village features rustic buildings designed to blend with the natural landscape. It includes an information center, hotels and lodges, a trailer park and campgrounds, a shopping plaza, a museum, and other tourist facilities and attractions. Grand Canyon Village, begun in the 1920s, is the largest tourist "town" ever developed by the National Park Service. It is considered an outstanding example of town planning. The village is divided into residential, commercial, civic, and historic areas, with a central plaza. Designated a National Historic Landmark in 1997.

### ❖ GRAND CANYON ❖

- 🌿 The canyon covers about 904 square miles (4,931 square kilometers).
- 🌿 It is about 277 miles (446 kilometers) long.
- 🌿 Its deepest point is about 5,000 feet (1,524 meters).
- 🌿 Its widest point is about 18 miles (29 kilometers).
- 🌿 Located in western Arizona, which is bordered by California, Nevada, Utah, Colorado, New Mexico, and the Mexican state of Sonora

## TOMBSTONE

**TOMBSTONE HISTORIC DISTRICT** One of the best-preserved frontier towns of the 1880s. Site of one of the richest silver strikes in the West, Tombstone was typical of the rugged lawlessness of the frontier. Ed Schieffelin, a prospector, settled it in 1879. His silver strike attracted thousands of miners and gamblers, and shootings were common. Main tourist attractions include the O.K. Corral, site of the legendary gunfight between the lawmen Virgil and Wyatt Earp and the gun-slinging Clanton gang; Boothill Graveyard, named for the men who "died with their boots on"; and the Bird Cage Theatre. The town's heyday as a mining center ended with the flooding of the silver mines in the early 1900s. Designated a National Historic Landmark in 1962.

### ❖ TOMBSTONE ❖

- 🌿 First settled by Americans from the eastern United States in 1879 after silver was discovered
- 🌿 Located in southeastern Arizona
- 🌿 Site of a historic silver-mining town
- 🌿 Nicknamed "The Town Too Tough to Die"

**LOWELL OBSERVATORY** Arizona's first astronomical observatory, founded in 1894 on Mars Hill in Flagstaff. An astronomer, Percival Lowell, established it to look for evidence of intelligent life on Mars. Several important discoveries have been made at the observatory, including Pluto in 1930. The observatory is still in operation today. Designated a National Historic Landmark in 1965.

**SAN XAVIER DEL BAC MISSION** Historic Jesuit mission south of Tucson, considered to be one of the finest examples of Spanish mission architecture in the United States. Father Eusebio Francisco Kino founded it in 1700 to convert the Papago people to Christianity and to teach them new farming methods. The church, built of stone and brick and covered with white plaster, dates to 1797. It is known as the "White Dove of the Desert" for its graceful Baroque features and white exterior. A major restoration was completed in 1997, and the mission is still an active parish today. Designated a National Historic Landmark in 1960.

# ARKANSAS

## LITTLE ROCK

**LITTLE ROCK CENTRAL HIGH SCHOOL** Site of a historic confrontation in the American civil rights movement in 1957. Completed in 1908, the secondary school is still thriving in downtown Little Rock. The brick and concrete building remains a symbol of the battle for racial integration in the United States.

HISTORY The 1954 United States Supreme Court decision *Brown v. Board of Education* outlawed racial segregation in public schools and set the stage for the events in Little Rock. In the summer of 1957, the city school board agreed to admit nine African American students to the all-white Little Rock Central High School. But the Arkansas governor, Orval

❖ **LITTLE ROCK** ❖

- First settled by Europeans in 1722
- Located on the Arkansas River in central Arkansas
- State capital of Arkansas, which is bordered by Tennessee, Mississippi, Louisiana, Texas, Oklahoma, and Missouri
- Little Rock is the only state capital with three capitol buildings: the restored territorial capitol, the Old State House, and the present capitol.

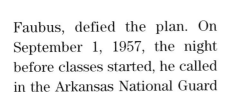

The racial confrontation at Little Rock Central High School in 1957 made national headlines. In 1997, President Bill Clinton and the "Little Rock Nine" commemorated the historic events of 40 years earlier. Today, the school serves about 2,000 students.

Faubus, defied the plan. On September 1, 1957, the night before classes started, he called in the Arkansas National Guard to surround the building and to prevent the African American students—called the "Little Rock Nine"—from entering the school.

On September 20, a federal judge ruled that the National Guard could not be used to stop integration and ordered the unit to be removed. When school resumed on Monday, September 23, an angry mob waited outside to block the students. Police escorted the teens quietly through a side door. When the crowd learned that the students were inside, it grew angry. The violence worsened, and police ushered the students away.

The following day, President Dwight Eisenhower sent federal troops to Little Rock. On September 25, the nine black students were escorted back into the school by armed guards. Under federal protection, they finished out the school year. One graduated that May.

In the fall of 1958, however, Governor Faubus closed the city's high schools. Students were forced to take correspondence courses or move away. The school board reopened the schools in 1959. Despite several incidents of violence, four of the original "Little Rock Nine" returned. Permanent integration had been achieved.

TODAY Nearly 2,000 students attend Little Rock Central High School. A majority are African American. A museum and visitor center was opened next door in 1997. Designated a unit of the National Park Service in 1998.

❖ PARKIN ❖

🐾 A town located on the St. Francis River in eastern Arkansas

🐾 Site of Parkin Archeological State Park

🐾 The childhood home of author Bette Green, whose young-adult novels include *Summer of My German Soldier* (1971)

## PARKIN

**PARKIN INDIAN MOUND** Archaeological site in a 17-acre (6.9-hectare) Native American village, dating from A.D. 1000 to 1550, on the St. Francis River in eastern Arkansas. The flat-topped mound is believed to have been the foundation of a temple or chief's residence in the prehistoric culture archaeologists call "Late Mississippian." Six smaller, surrounding mounds—perhaps supporting the residences of other important leaders—have also been identified. Some scholars believe that the Spanish explorer Hernando de Soto visited the village, referred to as Casqui, in 1541.

Excavations, which began in 1967, can be observed by visitors today. A research center and museum are also located in the state park. Designated a National Historic Landmark in 1964.

## MORE SITES

**BATH HOUSE ROW** A grouping of eight bathhouses in the town of Hot Springs that reflects the popularity of the spa movement of the nineteenth and early twentieth centuries. People went to the bathhouses to soak in the warm water and to improve their health. The buildings are noted for their elaborate architectural ornamentation. One still operates as a bathhouse, and another as a museum. Designated a National Historic Landmark in 1987.

**FORT SMITH** United States military outpost built in 1817 at the confluence of the Arkansas and Poteau Rivers near the OKLAHOMA border. One of the first federal garrisons in the Missouri Territory, it was established to control Native Americans in the area. Also located at the site are an old commissary, or store, the jail, and a national cemetery. Designated a National Historic Landmark in 1960.

# CALIFORNIA

## COLOMA

**SUTTER'S MILL** Site in the Sacramento Valley where gold was discovered on January 24, 1848, setting off the California gold rush. The initial strike was made at John Sutter's sawmill on the South Fork of the American River. Beginning in 1849, thousands of easterners poured into northern California to prospect for ore, leading to the greatest series of gold strikes in North America. Called "Forty-niners," about 80,000 settlers and prospectors came to these fields, living a rough-and-tumble life made famous in Hollywood movies. The nearby town of Coloma became a trading center for the regional mining camps. It died not long after the gold mines were emptied in the late 1850s. Today, the restored Sutter's Mill and its surrounding areas are part of a state park. Designated a National Historic Landmark in 1961.

## SAN DIEGO

### SAN DIEGO MISSION CHURCH
Mission San Diego de Alcalá, the oldest Spanish mission in California. Father Junípero Serra, a Franciscan friar, or priest, dedicated it on July 16, 1769. It was the first in a chain of 21 California missions sponsored by Spain and the Roman Catholic Church. The Spanish, who had colonized Mexico, sought to control lands to the north, and the Catholic Church wanted to convert Native Americans to Christianity. The mission was named for Saint Didacus of Alcalá, a Spanish Franciscan who dedicated his life to educating and caring for the sick.

### ❖ COLOMA ❖

🌿 First settled by Europeans in the 1840s and named for a nearby Native American village

🌿 A village located in eastern California, which is bordered by Oregon, Nevada, Arizona, the Pacific Ocean, and the Mexican states of Sonora and Baja California

🌿 Site of the discovery that triggered the California gold rush (1849)

Mission San Diego de Alcalá's architecture is typical of all the Spanish-built missions in California.

The original mission and its *presidio*, or fort, were built on a hill overlooking San Diego, but it was moved several times because Native Americans who did not want the Spanish on their land attacked it. The mission was finally relocated to its present site, 5 miles (8.0 kilometers) up the San Diego River, in 1774. The present buildings were completed in 1813, but the mission fell into decline in the 1820s. The church and its surrounding structures, which had deteriorated to ruins, were restored to their original beauty in the 1930s. In 1941, the mission once again became an active Catholic parish, which continues to serve San Diego today. Designated a National Historic Landmark in 1970.

### ❖ SAN DIEGO ❖

- Located in southwestern California, on the Pacific Ocean
- First settled by the Spanish in 1769
- Site of the first European settlement and oldest Spanish mission in California
- San Diego is home to one of the largest United States Navy installations on the West Coast. Its fleet ranges from aircraft carriers to atomic submarines.

### ★ PROFILE ★
## FATHER JUNÍPERO SERRA

A Spanish priest of the Roman Catholic Franciscan order, Father Serra went with a military expedition to Alto (Upper) California in 1769 and founded nine missions between what are now San Diego and San Francisco. A total of 21 missions, devoted to converting the Native Americans to Christianity and to teaching them new farming methods, were eventually established in California. Although many Native Americans resisted—sometimes violently—Father Serra is believed to have personally baptized more than 6,000 people. His missionary work earned him the title "Apostle of California." He was beatified (declared "Blessed") by Pope John Paul II in 1988.

### SAN FRANCISCO

**U.S. IMMIGRATION STATION, ANGEL ISLAND** Located in San Francisco Bay near the Tiburon Peninsula, a U.S. immigration station that processed about 1 million people arriving from Asia between 1910 and 1940. Many of the immigrants, especially those from China and Japan, were held in barracks for weeks or months until their paperwork was processed. Later, because of prejudice against Asian immigrants, the Chinese Exclusion Act of 1882 limited the number of Chinese laborers allowed into the United States. The Immigration Acts of 1917 and 1924 severely restricted arrivals from Japan and other Asian countries.

Angel Island is the largest island in San Francisco Bay. During World War II (1941–1945), it was used as a prisoner-of-war camp.

- Englishman Sir Francis Drake first visited the area in 1759, but he landed north of the present-day city.
- First settled by the Spanish in 1776
- Located on the Pacific Coast, surrounding San Francisco Bay

During their weeks of detention, many Chinese carved poems in the barrack walls. Many of the poems can still be seen. They tell of the immigrants' hardships and their cultural pride. As much as Ellis Island in NEW YORK came to symbolize the immigration experience of Europeans arriving on the East Coast, so too Angel Island stands as a powerful symbol of the Asian American heritage of the West. Today, Angel Island is accessible by ferry or private boat. A museum has been created in the old barracks. Special exhibits and presentations educate the public about Angel Island's history. Angel Island was designated a National Historic Landmark in 1971 and is part of the California State Park system.

## TRUCKEE

**DONNER CAMP** Site of one of the most terrible tragedies in the history of the American West. In the winter of 1846–1847, a group of 89 pioneers bound for California by wagon train was trapped by heavy snows near Truckee (now Donner) Lake in the High Sierras. Led by Jacob and George Donner, the party faced bitter cold and a food shortage. A small group set out on snowshoes to seek help, while the rest of the party remained behind in two winter camps. Starving and desperate, the snowbound pioneers resorted to cannibalism in order to survive. Relief expeditions arrived several months later, rescuing 40 of the original party.

Donner Memorial State Park is located where many of the party lost their lives. The site of one of the cabins is marked by a monument that stands 22 feet (6.7 meters) high—the same height as the snow in that terrible winter of 1846–1847. Excavations at the camp have helped historians piece together the tragic story of the Donner Party. Today, the park offers facilities for camping, picnicking, boating, fishing, and hiking. The history of the area and its people are depicted in the Emigrant Trail Museum at the park. Designated a National Historic Landmark in 1961.

## ❖ TRUCKEE ❖

- First settled by Europeans in 1863
- Located in the Sierra Nevada of northeastern California
- Founded as Coburn's Station for pioneers traveling over the Sierra Nevada pass, becoming a railroad and logging center later in the nineteenth century
- Truckee was the name of a legendary Paiute Indian chief who led the Stevens party, a group of immigrants from Missouri, over the pass in 1844.

## MORE SITES

### HEARST SAN SIMEON ESTATE

A mansion high on a hill in San Simeon, on the Pacific Coast south of San Francisco, built by the wealthy newspaper publisher William Randolph Hearst. Julia Morgan, one of the earliest female architects, designed the mansion. The main residence, begun in 1919 and still unfinished at Hearst's death in 1951, is lavishly furnished and decorated with imported art treasures.

The front of the mansion resembles a Spanish mission. The grounds cover hundreds of acres and once included a large animal preserve. Descendants of some of these animals—including zebras—still roam the grounds. Designated a National Historic Landmark in 1976.

### MANZANAR WAR RELOCATION CENTER

A camp in the desert of eastern California where 10,000 Japanese Americans were held during World War II. Under Executive Order 9066, issued by President Franklin D. Roosevelt in 1942, Japanese Americans on the Pacific Coast could be detained as a security measure to prevent sabotage and spying. Without being accused of any crime or given a trial, they were removed from their homes and kept at Manzanar and other camps for up to four years. Established as a National Historic Site in 1992.

### SAN FRANCISCO CABLE CARS

A popular tourist attraction and unofficial symbol of the city of San Francisco. Cable cars were first built in the city in 1873. Climbing the steep hills of the city's downtown area, the cable cars do not operate under their own power. The cars move by "gripping" and "ungripping" an underground steel cable. Designated as a National Historic Landmark in 1964.

# COLORADO

**PIKES PEAK** A 14,110-foot (4,300-meter) mountain in the southern Rockies west of Colorado Springs. It is named for Zebulon Montgomery Pike (1779–1813), a United States army officer and explorer who "discovered" the mountain in 1806. (The mountain was already well known to Native Americans and Spanish explorers.) For westward-bound pioneers in the early to mid-1800s, Pikes Peak was a symbol of the frontier as well as a real destination. The discovery of gold and other minerals in the area attracted many settlers. "Pikes Peak or Bust!" was the cry on many a wagon train. Today a cog railway, which is designed to operate on steep slopes with a cogged center rail to

### ❖ COLORADO SPRINGS ❖

- Settled by General William Palmer and the workers of the Denver and Rio Grande railway in 1871

- Located at the foot of Pikes Peak in central Colorado, which is bordered by Wyoming, Nebraska, Kansas, Oklahoma, New Mexico, and Utah

- Originally called "Fountain Colony," but renamed "Colorado Springs" because of its many mineral springs

- Grew to absorb Colorado City (also known as "El Dorado"), a gold-mining community settled in 1850

provide traction, and a toll road provide access to the summit. Designated a National Historic Landmark in 1961.

DURANGO

**DURANGO-SILVERTON NARROW GAUGE RAILROAD** A vital rail connection, opened in 1882, between the mining towns of Durango and Silverton in southwestern Colorado. (A narrow-gauge train runs on rails set closer together than those of standard railroads. Such tracks fit through the

The Durango-Silverton Railroad stretches for 45 miles (72.4 kilometers). It is one of the few surviving narrow-gauge railroads in the nation.

mountain passes.) The 45-mile (72.4-kilo-meters) line was built by the Denver and Rio Grande Railway to haul silver and gold ore from mines in Silverton to a smelter—a place for melting and refining—in Durango. As in many other Western locations, the railroad was critically important to the local economy. Mining in the area flourished for decades. The Durango-Silverton Railroad continues to operate today. Coal-fired steam locomotives carry passenger cars through the winding canyons of the scenic San Juan Mountains and San Juan National Forest. Designated a National Historic Landmark in 1961.

### ❖ DURANGO ❖

- Established in 1880 by the Denver and Rio Grande Railway
- Located in southwest Colorado on the Animas River, near the Southern Ute Indian reservation
- Headquarters for San Juan National Forest and gateway to Mesa Verde National Park

## MORE SITES

### TELLURIDE HISTORIC DISTRICT

Once a rich and bustling gold-mining town, founded in 1878. The town grew quickly after 1890, when the Denver and Rio Grande Railway arrived. Today, the town is a major tourist and skiing center that actively works to preserve its historic buildings and sites. Designated a National Historic Landmark in 1961.

# CONNECTICUT

## MYSTIC SEAPORT

**EMMA C. BERRY** Fishing sloop launched in 1866 at Noank, Connecticut. It is one of the last surviving examples of the American smack, a once-popular sailing vessel with an internal wet well to keep the fish alive until reaching port. Its sleek design made the smack look more like a pleasure boat than a working fishing vessel. Sloops of this kind fished the waters off

The *Emma C. Berry* underwent major restoration in the 1930s and 1971.

the Atlantic Coast from MAINE to FLORIDA. Named for its captain's daughter, the *Emma* was used chiefly for catching mackerel. Today, it is a floating exhibit at the Mystic Seaport Museum. Designated a National Historic Landmark in 1994.

## ❖ MYSTIC SEAPORT ❖

- Active in shipbuilding as early as the sixteenth century, the seaport became a busy whaling center in the 1800s.

- Located on the southern coast of Connecticut, which is bordered by New York, Massachusetts, Rhode Island, Long Island Sound, and Block Island Sound

- The original maritime museum was created in 1929. Today, the restored village includes some 60 buildings and 200 ships and boats.

- Also known for its Mystic Aquarium

## NEW HAVEN

**NEW HAVEN GREEN HISTORIC DISTRICT** Grassy public square located in downtown New Haven. The Green is most noteworthy for three churches built there between 1812 and 1816. Located in a row at the center of the Green, or Common, and facing southeast, each of the three churches displays a different façade to the public. Together, they form a pleasing example of nineteenth-century urban design. The Center Church (First Church of Christ, Congregational) and United Church (Old North Church, Congregational) are both late Georgian/early Federal in style. Trinity Church (Episcopal) is an early example of the use of Gothic (or Medieval) detail in a church. Designated a National Historic Landmark in 1970.

## ❖ NEW HAVEN ❖

- Founded by English Puritans

- Site of Yale University, founded in 1701

- New Haven was one of the earliest communities to use a grid plan—like a checkerboard—with a common at the center.

## MORE SITES

**MARK TWAIN HOME** A large house in Hartford that was the residence of Samuel Langhorne Clemens from 1874 to 1891 and where he wrote many of his books. The house has many porches, towers, colors, materials, and forms, and has been described as "part steamboat, part medieval stronghold, and part cuckoo clock." Designated a National Historic Landmark in 1962. *See also* LOUISIANA, MISSOURI, NEVADA, and TENNESSEE.

**OLD STATE HOUSE** Located in Hartford, a Federal-style building that served as the capitol in the late 1700s and early 1800s. Designed by the well-known architect Charles Bullfinch in 1792, the building was completed in 1796. In 1814, representatives from the New England states met here at the Hartford Convention to discuss the possibility of seceding from the Union because of their opposition to the War of 1812. The building later became Hartford's city hall. Designated a National Historic Landmark in 1960.

# DELAWARE

## NEWARK

**IRON HILL SCHOOL NO. 112** A one-room schoolhouse for African American children built in 1923 in rural northern Delaware. In 1919, the state of Delaware had passed a law that required school attendance by all African American children younger than the age of 14. The industrialist Pierre S. du Pont contributed the money to build schools for them. Iron Hill was one of more than 80 such schools built between 1919 and 1928. These modest, single-teacher schools accommodated about 40 students. Iron Hill operated until 1965. Listed in the National Register of Historic Places in 1995.

### ❖ NEWARK ❖

🐾 First settled by the Dutch in 1655

🐾 Located in northwestern Delaware, which is bordered by Pennsylvania, New Jersey, Maryland, Delaware Bay, and the Atlantic Ocean

🐾 Site of the only revolutionary battle on Delaware soil

**FORT CHRISTINA** Site of the first Swedish military outpost, built in 1638, in the Delaware Valley. It was the commercial center of the first permanent Swedish settlement in North America, now the city of Wilmington.

A sculpture of the ship that carried the Swedes to Delaware was unveiled during the 1938 commemoration ceremonies at Fort Christina. The ceremonies were attended by thousands of people, including the crown prince of Sweden and President Franklin D. Roosevelt.

HISTORY The fort was built under the direction of Peter Minuit (1580–1638). Minuit was a Dutchman who was then working for the New Sweden Company. He bought the land, located on the western banks of the Delaware, from Native Americans. The fort, named in honor of the queen of Sweden, marked the beginning of the New Sweden colony.

The Dutch, who originally had financial interests in the New Sweden Company, soon withdrew from the colony. Swedish pioneers, who were more accustomed to cold winters and heavily forested land, succeeded in building up the colony and developing a fur trade. Under the leadership of Johan Björnsson Printz, the governor from 1643 to 1653, New Sweden thrived. It occupied parts of what is now southern NEW JERSEY, the area near Philadelphia, PENNSYLVANIA, and northern Delaware.

In 1655, the Dutch under Peter Stuyvesant sent troops and took control of the area. New Sweden was made part of the Dutch colony of New Netherland. The English, meanwhile, believed that the Dutch were interfering with their trade. In 1664, they sent out an attack fleet and conquered New Netherland. All of its land, including the former Swedish colony, was made part of NEW YORK. Fort Christina fell into disrepair, and the last remains eventually disappeared.

TODAY In 1938, 300 years after the fort was built, the site was opened as a state park. Special attractions include the "Rocks," the location on the Christina River where the Swedes landed in 1638, and a large sculpture of the *Kalmar Nyckel*, the ship that carried them. Designated a National Historic Landmark in 1961.

## ❖ WILMINGTON ❖

- Settled by the Quakers William and Elizabeth Shipley in 1638; bought by William Penn in 1682
- Located in northeast Delaware at the mouth of Christina River and Brandywine Creek
- The largest city in Delaware and a busy shipping port
- More than half of the nation's Fortune 500 companies are incorporated in Wilmington

## MORE SITES

ELEUTHERIAN MILLS Gunpowder mill established in 1802–1803 by Eleuthère Irenée du Pont on Brandywine Creek near Wilmington. The mill produced explosive powders used by the United States military for more than 100 years. It marked the beginning of the giant E.I. du Pont Company. Designated a National Historic Landmark in 1966.

LOMBARDY HALL The home of Gunning Bedford, Jr., a Delaware delegate to the Continental Congress and a signer of the United States Constitution. Bedford lived in the granite house from 1793 until 1812. Located in Wilmington, it is now a museum. Designated a National Historic Landmark in 1974.

# FLORIDA

CAPE CANAVERAL

**CAPE CANAVERAL AIR FORCE STATION** The launching area for the American space program, selected by the Air Force in 1947. Rockets were tested and launched from the Cape during the late 1940s and 1950s. The area's importance grew after the Soviet Union launched *Sputnik I*, the world's first artificial satellite, in 1957.

On May 25, 1961, President John F. Kennedy announced that the United States would send astronauts to the Moon and return them safely to Earth by the end of the 1960s. Throughout the decade Mercury, Gemini,

### ❖ CAPE CANAVERAL ❖

- Explored by the Spaniard Ponce de León in 1513
- Sparsely populated until the growth of the NASA space program in the late 1950s, the town was incorporated around 1960.
- Located in east-central Florida, which is bordered by Alabama, Georgia, the Atlantic Ocean, and the Gulf of Mexico
- Cape Canaveral Air Force Station launched the first United States space satellite (1958), the first American to orbit Earth (1962), and the first man on the Moon (1969).

## ★ PROFILE ★
## FRANKLIN CHANG-DIAZ

The first Hispanic American in space. Born in Costa Rica in 1950, Chang-Diaz moved to the United States and received his doctorate degree in applied physics from the Massachusetts Institute of Technology (MIT) in 1977. Dr. Chang-Diaz became an astronaut in 1981 and has flown several space shuttle flights. Chang-Diaz has developed many scientific concepts, including new ideas on rocket propulsion that may be useful on future missions to Mars. In addition to his main areas of science and physics, Chang-Diaz was an instructor for a community rehabilitation program for Hispanics for more than two years. Dr. Chang-Diaz is married and has four children.

Space shuttle flights began lifting off from Cape Canaveral in 1981.

and Apollo missions were launched from Cape Canaveral. Finally on July 20, 1969, *Apollo 11* fulfilled President Kennedy's dream—three astronauts reached the Moon and returned safely. Apollo missions carried astronauts to the Moon and back until 1972.

Today, Cape Canaveral is the launch site for space shuttles, missiles, and rockets. Designated (selected areas) a National Historic Landmark in 1984. *See also* TEXAS.

## ST. AUGUSTINE

**ST. AUGUSTINE TOWN PLAN HISTORIC DISTRICT** Founded in 1565, the oldest continuously inhabited city in the continental United States. Spanish explorers, under orders from King Phillip II, established the town of St. Augustine to help protect treasure ships as they passed near the coast of Florida. The city is like an old Spanish settlement, with narrow streets leading from a central plaza.

St. Augustine became part of the United States in 1821 when Spain sold East Florida. Americans became interested in the area after the Civil War ended in 1865. Henry M. Flagler, a cofounder of Standard Oil, built luxury hotels in St. Augustine as well as railroads to bring rich northerners to his winter resorts. Efforts to preserve the historic colonial buildings began in the 1950s and continue today. Designated a National Historic Site in 1970.

## MORE SITES

**ERNEST HEMINGWAY HOUSE** Home of the famous writer Ernest Hemingway from 1931 to 1940. Located in Key West, the house was built in the mid-1800s from limestone quarried on the site, which was then covered by stucco. Iron verandas surround the house on all sides, and large windows allow tropical breezes to cool the house. Today, it is a museum honoring Hemingway and his writings. Designated a National Historic Landmark in 1968.

**FORT WALTON MOUND** An ancient Indian site, dating back to about A.D. 1200 and believed to be part of the Middle Mississippian culture. The earliest people, however, probably lived at the site in the first century A.D. Located in North Florida, the site was excavated in 1901. Designated a National Historic Landmark in 1964.

# GEORGIA

**ANDERSONVILLE NATIONAL HISTORIC SITE** Notorious Civil War prison in southwestern Georgia where Confederate forces confined more than 45,000 Union soldiers. Nearly 13,700 of them died from disease, starvation, or exposure to the elements during the 14 months of the prison's existence.

HISTORY Officially called Camp Sumter, the Andersonville stockade was built in February 1864 to keep large numbers of Union prisoners previously held near Richmond, VIRGINIA. The 16-acre (6.5-hectare) facility was originally designed for 10,000 prisoners but quickly became overcrowded. It was expanded to 26 acres (10.5 hectares) and accommodated a peak of 33,000 men in August 1864. Because there were no barracks, prisoners lived in floorless tents. One meagerly supplied clinic provided medical care. Poor sanitation, malnutrition, and brutal heat

Almost 13,000 Union soldiers who died in the Andersonville prison are buried in the national cemetery, which was established in February 1865 and is pictured above.

during the summer months caused the deaths of more than one hundred Union soldiers every day.

The federal government and Union newspapers vehemently protested the treatment of prisoners at Andersonville. At some Northern stockades, rebel captives received harsh treatment in retaliation. Finally in January 1865, the Confederates agreed to exchange several thousand Union prisoners for their own men who were held in the North. The final liberation of Andersonville came with the end of the Civil War in April 1865. The prison superintendent, Captain Henry Wirz, was later tried and executed for war crimes.

TODAY The National Andersonville Historic Site is a 495-acre (200-hectare) park dedicated to American prisoners of war throughout the nation's history. It includes the site of the original prison and a national cemetery for those who died there. In 1998, the National Prisoners of War Museum was opened to commemorate the hundreds of thousands of American men and women who suffered captivity in the nation's armed conflicts. The architecture, displays, and presentations describe the prisoner-of-war experience since the American Revolution. Designated as a National Historic Site in 1970.

🐝 Located in Macon County in south-western Georgia, which is bordered by Tennessee, North Carolina, South Carolina, Florida, and the Atlantic Ocean

🐝 Before the infamous prison was built in 1864, the town had a population of fewer than 20.

🐝 The first archaeological excavations of the prison began in 1987.

## ATLANTA

**STATE CAPITOL** Monumental limestone building at the center of a complex of state, county, and city offices in downtown Atlanta. Designed in the Roman

Although the capitol was completed in 1889, gold was not applied to the dome until a 1957 restoration. All the gold on the dome is from Georgia.

classical style, recalling the U.S. capitol in WASHINGTON, D.C., and other government buildings, the building features a gold dome measuring 75 feet (22.8 meters) in diameter and a portico supported by six large Corinthian columns. Built between 1884 and 1889, the building became a symbol of Atlanta's identity as capital of the "New South" after Reconstruction. Unlike most other state capitols, it was completed for less than the amount budgeted—$1 million. Major repairs and renovations were undertaken after a chunk of ceiling fell to the floor in 1995. Designated a National Historic Landmark in 1973.

❖ A T L A N T A ❖

- Founded in 1837 as "Terminus" (because it was the end of a railroad line) on land occupied by the Creek Indians
- Located in northwest Georgia near the Appalachian foothills
- Largest city and state capital of Georgia
- Captured by Union General William Tecumseh Sherman in 1864 and almost entirely destroyed by fire

founded the Warm Springs Foundation for the care of polio victims. During his presidency (1933–1945), Roosevelt's home at Warm Springs became known as the "Little White House." He died there in April 1945. The treatment facility, later renamed the Roosevelt Warm Springs Institute for Rehabilitation, now serves patients with a variety of physical disabilities. Designated a National Historic Landmark in 1980.

## WARM SPRINGS

### WARM SPRINGS HISTORIC DISTRICT

A small resort town in western Georgia, where Franklin D. Roosevelt took relief from polio in natural mineral waters. The springs, which remain at a constant temperature of 88°F (31°C), became the site of a resort town in 1830. Roosevelt began visiting in 1924, three years after being stricken by the disease. In 1927, he

## MORE SITES

**SAVANNAH HISTORIC DISTRICT** The original residential section of Georgia's oldest city and largest seaport on the Atlantic Coast. Planned by James Oglethorpe in 1733, the beautifully preserved grid of streets features parklike public squares and hundreds of historic houses and churches. Designated a National Historic Landmark in 1966.

**FOX THEATRE** Located in Atlanta, a large and ornate movie house that opened in 1929. Known as the "Fabulous Fox," the theater is designed in a neo-Moorish style, with onion domes, arched windows, and towers known as minarets. The main auditorium, planned as a courtyard, continues the Arabian theme. The theater is still used for movie revivals and live shows. Designated a National Historic Landmark in 1976.

❖ W A R M   S P R I N G S ❖

- Settled in the 1830s as a mineral springs resort community
- A town located in western Georgia
- According to legend, Native Americans also used the warm springs for healing, and a wounded warrior on his way to the springs could pass safely through hostile territories.

# HAWAII

## HONOLULU

**IOLANI PALACE** Official residence of the last monarchs of the Kingdom of Hawaii. Known as "the only royal palace under the American flag," Iolani Palace was home to King Kalakaua (reigned 1874–1891) and Queen Liliuokalani (reigned 1891–1893). It is an impressive and enduring symbol of the days of Hawaiian independence.

The ornate structure, built between 1879 and 1882, combines Italian and French architectural design elements. It features two stories of arched verandas suited to Hawaii's warm climate. The first floor of the building was used for formal functions. The second floor served as living quarters for the royal family.

### ★ PROFILE ★
### QUEEN LILIUOKALANI

The last queen of Hawaii, she was originally named Lydia Kamekeha. Liliuokalani succeeded her brother, King Kalakaua, to the throne in 1891. Two years later, she was overthrown by American sugar growers who established the Republic of Hawaii. She officially abdicated in 1895. A talented songwriter, Liliuokalani also wrote the popular "Aloha Oe" ("Farewell to Thee").

### ❖ HONOLULU ❖

- First settled by Europeans in 1820, when missionaries arrived from New England

- State capital of Hawaii, which includes 132 Pacific islands about 2,400 miles (3,862 kilometers) west of San Francisco. Major islands are Hawaii, Maui, Kahoolawe, Lanai, Molokai, Oahu, Kauai, and Niihau.

- Located on southeast Oahu, Honolulu is the crossroads of the Pacific, with cruise ship and air connections to the U.S. mainland, Asia, Australia, and New Zealand.

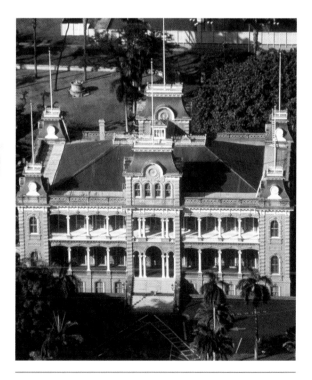

An extensive renovation of Iolani Palace began in 1969 at a cost of $6 million. It took nine years to restore the palace to its original beauty.

Kitchens, storerooms, and household staff occupied the basement.

In 1898, when the United States annexed the Hawaiian Islands, the official transfer of power took place at Iolani Palace. The ceremony was held on the King Street steps on August 12, 1898. The building also served as capitol for the territory and the state of Hawaii until the new state capitol was completed in 1969. Today, it houses a museum devoted to the history and culture of Hawaii. Designated a National Historic Landmark in 1962.

## PEARL HARBOR

**USS *ARIZONA* MEMORIAL** U.S. Navy battleship sunk in Pearl Harbor during

- The Japanese attack on Pearl Harbor crippled the American fleet in less than three hours.
- Eight battleships were damaged, and five were sunk during the attack.
- As a result of the attack, 2,335 servicemen and women were killed, 68 civilians died, and 1,178 people were wounded.

the Japanese surprise attack on December 7, 1941. Photographs of the burning ship appeared on the front pages of newspapers across the country. For generations of Americans, the sinking of the *Arizona* has symbolized the destruction of the Pacific Fleet at Pearl Harbor and the start of World War II.

The 31,400-ton battleship was launched in 1915 at the New York Navy Yard. On the morning of December 7, 1941, the *Arizona* was moored off Ford Island, Pearl Harbor, when Japanese bombers flooded the sky. The ship sustained eight hits. One of them struck a powder magazine, where gunpowder and other ammunitions were stored, causing other explosions and devastating fires. The *Arizona* sank in its dock. A total of 1,177 sailors and marines on the *Arizona* were killed—about half of all those lost that fateful Sunday.

The USS *Arizona* exploded when it was hit by a 1,760-pound armor-piercing bomb. The battleship sank in less than nine minutes.

The USS *Arizona* Memorial was opened in 1962 to commemorate the attack and to honor the military personnel who lost their lives. The 184-foot (56-meter) building straddles the midsection of the sunken hull. A shrine room contains a marble wall on which the names of those killed are engraved. A mast attached to the submerged ship carries an American flag. Designated a National Historic Landmark in 1989.

---

## MORE SITES

**KALAUPAPA LEPROSY SETTLEMENT** A peninsula on the north shore of the island of Molokai where a leper colony was established in 1866. An epidemic of leprosy, a contagious disease that causes severe deformities, had broken out among native Hawaiians. Joseph de Veuster, a Belgian Catholic priest, known as Father Damien, cared for the sick from 1873 until his death from the disease in 1889. Designated a National Historic Park in 1980.

**COOK LANDING SITE** The place where Captain James Cook, the first European known to have sighted the Hawaiian Islands, is believed to have set foot in 1778. Now a park, it is located on the southwestern coast of the island of Kauai. Designated a National Historic Landmark in 1962.

# IDAHO

## CATALDO

**CATALDO MISSION** The oldest mission church still standing in the Pacific Northwest. It is also the oldest building in Idaho today. Jesuit missionaries, called "blackrobes," who were seeking to convert Coeur d'Alene Native Americans to Catholicism, built the church in the early 1850s. The mission is located in Kootenai County in the far north of the state. It overlooks the Coeur d'Alene River from a small hill. The site was sacred to the local people of the area. The church was moved there from its original location in 1887.

First known as the Mission of the Sacred Heart, it was designed by an Italian Jesuit named Father Anthony Ravalli. Using local materials, he tried to fashion a building that resembled the cathedrals of his native country. The white, wood-framed structure features a front portico, or porch entrance, with six supporting

### ❖ CATALDO ❖

- Settled by Jesuit missionaries in 1820
- Located in northern Idaho, which is bordered by Montana, Wyoming, Utah, Nevada, Oregon, Washington, and the Canadian province of British Columbia
- Named after Father Joseph M. Cataldo, Superior of the Rocky Mountain Jesuit missions (1877–1893)

columns. Above it, on the face of the exterior, is an Italian Baroque pediment that contains a beautiful sunburst decoration. Inside, the chandeliers were made from old tin cans, and the wood altar was painted to look like marble. The church is named for Father Joseph Cataldo, who arrived in 1877. Designated a National Historic Landmark in 1961.

## CITY OF ROCKS STATE PARK

**CITY OF ROCKS STATE PARK** A popular rest area and campsite for travelers on the California Trail from the 1840s to 1880s. Located in south-central Idaho, City of Rocks is named for its many granite outcroppings. Their shape bears a striking resemblance to a city skyline. Surrounded by vast sagebrush plains, the area's creeks and wooded mountainsides were a welcome sight to weary migrants. The ruts of wagon wheels can still be seen today, and the giant rocks bear names and inscriptions carved by many travelers. Designated a National Historic Landmark in 1964.

## ❖ CITY OF ROCKS STATE PARK ❖

- Named for the rocks that appear to form an urban skyline
- Is managed jointly by the National Park Service and the Idaho Department of Parks

### MORE SITES

**FORT HALL** Built in 1834 and now part of a Native American Reservation in the Snake River Valley. It was an important supply center for pioneers on the Oregon and California trails. Designated a National Historic Landmark in 1961.

**LEMHI PASS** A high mountain pass in the Beaverhead Range where explorers Lewis and Clark crossed the Continental Divide in August 1805. At the time, it formed the boundary between the newly acquired Louisiana Territory and Spanish lands to the west. Today, it marks the border between Idaho and MONTANA. Designated a National Historic Landmark in 1960.

The above photo shows some of the granite peaks of the City of Rocks State Park. They are thought to be 2.5 million years old. Today, park visitors enjoy camping and rock climbing.

# ILLINOIS

## CHICAGO

**FREDERICK C. ROBIE HOUSE** A prairie-style home, designed and built between 1906 and 1909 by Frank Lloyd Wright for Frederick C. Robie, a wealthy Midwestern bicycle manufacturer. It is considered to be one of the most important examples of twentieth-century residential architecture. The prairie-style home is uniquely American.

Wright created prairie-style homes, which hug the earth and echo the flat Midwestern landscape with their horizontal form. These homes use natural colors, and the decoration is integral to the form. Inside the homes, rooms are large and bright. A unique characteristic of the Robie House is a stretch of 174 decorative art glass windows, which take advantage of the sun's path to let in light. As he often did, Wright designed most of the furniture in the home, since he considered the furnishings to be an extension of his overall design of the house.

Renovation of the Robie House, which is owned by the University of Chicago, began in 1999 and is expected to cost more than $7 million. Upon completion, it will be opened to the public as a museum. Designated a National Historic Landmark in 1963.

- Explorers Father Jacques Marquette and Louis Joliet were the first Europeans to visit the site of present-day Chicago.

- Jean Baptiste Point du Sable, an African American from Haiti, became the first permanent resident in 1779.

- Organized as a city in 1837

- The 1871 Great Chicago Fire destroyed 2,124 acres (859.5 hectares) of land and about 17,540 buildings; more than 98,000 people were left homeless.

## COLLINSVILLE

**CAHOKIA MOUNDS** The site of an early Native American culture, known as the Mississippian Moundbuilders, dating from about A.D. 800 to 1500. This early civilization disappeared just about the time European exploration began.

Cahokia was the largest of the Mississippian Moundbuilders' cities. In the thirteenth century, it had a population of about 30,000—larger than any European city of the time. The people built huge earthen mounds that served as religious and governmental centers. Monks Mound, the largest in Cahokia, was one-fourth larger than the Great Pyramid of Gaza in Egypt.

The Moundbuilders left no written records of their civilization. By studying the pottery, arrowheads, jewelry, and other artifacts of this people, archaeologists have learned that this was a powerful and highly organized society. Most of

Monks Mound, the largest eastern mound in Cahokia, towered more than 100 feet (30.4 meters) into the air. It has been frequently repaired and reconstructed by the native people.

the people were farmers who grew corn, beans, and squash. These crops, plus the game the people hunted, allowed them to live in year-round settlements and, in turn, led to a culture that produced goods that could be traded with other nearby communities.

Today, archaeologists are still studying the mounds at Cahokia to find out more about these prehistoric people. Recent excavations have discovered a stockade, or wall, built around the central part of the city. Another find included 70 unused stone axes—each about 1,000 years old.

Much of the area of the mounds is now part of Cahokia Mounds State Park. Designated a National Historic Landmark in 1964.

## PRINCETON

**OWEN LOVEJOY HOUSE** A station on the Underground Railroad and the home of the abolitionist and Congregationalist minister, Owen Lovejoy. The home was built in the 1830s. A two-story wooden structure, the house has 15 rooms. The Lovejoy family hid escaped slaves in one of six rooms on the second floor until the slaves could move on to the next station—and eventually to Canada and freedom.

Lovejoy preached his fiery abolitionist views in his church sermons. In 1856, as the nation moved closer toward civil war, he was elected to the House of Representatives, where he served five terms. He became known across the nation for his work to end slavery. Today, the Owen Lovejoy House is a museum. Designated a National Historic Landmark in 1997.

## SPRINGFIELD

**LINCOLN HOME** Home of the sixteenth president of the United States and his family from 1844 until 1861, at the time they moved to WASHINGTON, D.C. The only home the Lincolns ever owned, it was restored to its 1860 appearance in 1988.

The Lincolns bought their Greek-revival style home in 1844 for $1,200 and a land lot worth about $300. In 1856, they expanded the second floor because they needed the room for their growing family. All four of the Lincoln's children were born in the house, and one, Edward, died there

in 1850. Lincoln learned of his presidential nomination in 1860 in the home's parlor.

After Lincoln won the election, the home was the center of celebrations and political rallies. As the Lincolns prepared to move to WASHINGTON, D.C., they sold most of their furniture, gave the family dog to a neighbor, and rented the house.

The Lincolns' only surviving son, Robert Todd Lincoln, gave the home to the state of Illinois in 1887. He asked that visitors' admission to the house be free. Today, the home, located in downtown Springfield, and the surrounding four blocks are much as they were in 1860, complete with wooden plank sidewalks. Established as a National Historic Site in 1971. *See also* KENTUCKY, OHIO, and WISCONSIN.

The parlor of the Lincoln home has been restored to look much like it was when the Lincolns lived there.

❖ **SPRINGFIELD** ❖

- The first European settlers, John and Mary Kelley, arrived in 1819
- State capital of Illinois
- Lincoln's tomb was dedicated in 1874, nine years after his burial.

## MORE SITES

**CHICAGO AVENUE WATER TOWER AND PUMPING STATION** Completed in 1869, the Water Tower survived the Great Chicago Fire of 1871. The tower is built of limestone quarried in nearby Joliet. Today, the Water Tower stands in the middle of busy Michigan Avenue in downtown Chicago and is an official welcome center for the city. Listed in the National Register of Historic Places in 1975.

**GRANT PARK STADIUM (SOLDIER FIELD)** Located on Chicago's lakefront, the stadium is popularly known as Soldier Field. It opened in 1924 as a memorial to World War I (1914–1918) soldiers. At the time, it was one of the largest stadiums in the world and was designed to be used for many types of events. Since 1971, it has been the home of the Chicago Bears. A massive renovation to modernize the stadium began in 2002. Designated a National Historic Landmark in 1987.

# INDIANA

## INDIANAPOLIS

**MADAME C.J. WALKER MANUFAC-TURING COMPANY** Completed in 1927, the hub of the first female African American millionaire's hair-care and cosmetic business. Walker's operation became the most successful African American-owned business at the time. She employed about 3,000 women.

**HISTORY** Born in Louisiana in 1867, Sarah Breedlove was the daughter of formerly enslaved African Americans. She was or-

phaned at age seven and married Moses McWilliams at fourteen. After Moses died in 1887, Sarah and her two-year-old daughter moved to St. Louis, Missouri. There, she scraped by as a washerwoman, earning about $1.50 a day.

In 1905, she discovered a successful hair-care formula for her own thinning hair. She started selling her products through local clubs and churches and later through mail order. Sarah McWilliams's products became popular with African American women who wanted to straighten their hair.

She married C.J. Walker in 1906, and following a custom of some businesswomen of the time, she added the title "Madame" to her name. As her business expanded, she hired other African American women. They became known as "Walker Agents" and sold her products door to door.

In 1910, she moved her operation to Indianapolis, an urban transportation hub with a thriving African American community. She revolutionized the hair-care industry at a time when segregation

### ❖ INDIANAPOLIS ❖

- State capital of Indiana, which is bordered by Ohio, Kentucky, Illinois, Michigan, and Lake Michigan
- Selected as the site of Indiana's capital in 1821
- Became a thriving auto manufacturing center in the early 1900s
- Joined in 1970 with Marion County to create one city-county government

was legal and women were denied the same rights as men. She provided work for African American women who would otherwise have worked in menial jobs for little money.

Walker became one of the richest women in America and donated thousands of dollars to charities and schools. She died in 1919 at the age of 51. About two-thirds of her $2 million estate went to charity.

TODAY Madame Walker planned the four-story Walker Building in Indianapolis, but it was completed after her death. The building served as the business's headquarters and as a social center for the African American community. Restored in the 1980s, today it houses the Madame Walker Theater Center and other businesses. Designated a National Historic Landmark in 1991.

LAFAYETTE

**TIPPECANOE BATTLEFIELD** Located seven miles north of Lafayette, the site of a victory over the Shawnee by about 1,000 American troops in 1811. Tecumseh, a Native American leader, together with his brother, known as "The Prophet," planned to unite the many tribes of the area and defend the land from the white settlers.

The Americans, under General William Henry Harrison, marched into the wilderness to confront the Native Americans. Despite Tecumseh's warning to delay fighting the whites until the tribes were ready, "The Prophet" attacked. About two hours later, the Native Americans were crushed.

In 1840, the Whig party nominated Harrison for president. To take advantage of his military career, the Whigs held a huge rally at the Tippecanoe battlefield. The campaign slogan "Tippecanoe and Tyler, too!" refers to the hero of the Battle of Tippecanoe and to his running mate, John Tyler. Today, the battlefield is a county park. Reenactments of the battle are staged every November 7. Designated a National Historic Landmark in 1960.

Although the battle was fought in 1811, the 85-foot (25.9 meter) obelisk, or four-sided pillar, was not erected until 1908. The monument cost $24,500 and is pictured above.

❖ **LAFAYETTE** ❖

🌿 Settled by the French in the 1700s

🌿 Launch site of the first official air-mail flight by the United States Postal Service—by hot-air balloon in 1859

🌿 Purdue University founded in 1869

**EUGENE V. DEBS HOME** From 1890 to 1926, the Terre Haute home of the well-known industrial unionist and political leader. During his lifetime, many of Debs's social beliefs were unpopular. Today, the restored home is a memorial to Debs and his ideals. Designated a National Historic Landmark in 1966.

**INDIANAPOLIS MOTOR SPEEDWAY** Home of the Indianapolis 500, a car race held every year since 1911. It is the world's oldest continuously operating automobile racetrack. Today, a Hall of Fame Museum stands next to the track. Designated a National Historic Landmark in 1987.

# IOWA

## AMANA

**AMANA COLONIES** Seven communal villages founded as the Amana Church Society in 1855. Still a thriving production and marketing cooperative, the Amana Society was the most successful of many utopian, or idealistic, communities of the nineteenth century. It was established by the Community of True Inspiration, a religious sect that emphasized religious devotion, ethical purity, and charitable works. Some eight hundred members of this group left Germany in the early 1840s, settling first in NEW YORK and later moving to Iowa.

At first, all land and businesses in the settlement were the common property of members, which was managed by elders of the church. Eventually, the settlement grew to seven villages across 26,000 acres (10,500 hectares) along the Iowa River near Cedar Rapids. In 1932, religious and business affairs of the community were separated. Property and shares of the business could be privately owned. Today, the Amana Society continues to produce agricultural goods and kitchen appliances.

The religious organization, with some 500 members, also continues to practice. A number of buildings from the early years of the settlement are now used as gift shops, museums, and bed-and-breakfast lodgings for visitors. Designated a National Historic Landmark in 1965.

### ❖ AMANA COLONIES ❖

- Founded as the Amana Church Society in 1855 by a German religious sect
- Located in Iowa, which is bordered by Minnesota, Wisconsin, Illinois, Missouri, Nebraska, and South Dakota
- Includes seven communities: Amana, East Amana, West Amana, High Amana, Middle Amana, South Amana, and Homestead
- *Amana* means "remaining true" in German.

By the end of the nineteenth century, the Amana colonies were a successful and bustling group of village communities called "an Iowa treasure." The historic towns have been modernized and are a favorite tourist destination.

## WEST BRANCH

**HERBERT HOOVER BIRTHPLACE** A humble two-room cottage where the thirty-first president of the United States was born on August 10, 1874. The tiny wood-plank home, surrounded by a small yard and white picket fence, is located on Downey Street in the east-central Iowa town of West Branch. At the time, West Branch was a Quaker community. Hoover had a strict Quaker upbringing. Jesse, his father and the village blacksmith, built the cottage in 1870. He died when "Bertie," as the boy was nicknamed, was six. Hoover's mother Hulda died when he was 11. Bertie, his brother, and his sister then moved from West Branch to live with relatives.

Herbert Clark Hoover served as president of the United States from 1929 to 1933. His birthplace was restored in 1938 under his own direction. Today, the cottage contains some of his parents' original furnishings. It lies at the heart of a 200-acre (80-hectare) National Historic Site. Across the driveway stands the Hoover Presidential Library-Museum. Also located on the grounds are the graves of President Hoover and First Lady Lou Henry Hoover. Designated a National Historic Site in 1965.

🐾 The first settlers, including Herbert Hoover's grandfather, built homes along the "West Branch" of the Wapsinonoc Creek in the early 1850s.

🐾 A town located in eastern Iowa

🐾 Site of the West Branch Historic District, which contains sixteen buildings from the town's era of agricultural prosperity

## MORE SITES

**LINCOLN HIGHWAY** America's first cross-country highway, built and paved in the 1910s and early 1920s. In Iowa, as in most states through which it passed, the road was later renamed Route 30. The 358-mile (576-kilometer) stretch through Iowa was considered vital because it connected Chicago, ILLINOIS (to the east) and Omaha, NEBRASKA (to the west). Listed in the National Register of Historic Places in 1993.

**WOODBURY COUNTY COURTHOUSE** Located in Sioux City, the only major civic building designed in the prairie style. Constructed between 1916 and 1918, the four-story building is covered with Roman brick and terra-cotta trim. An eight-story tower rises from the center of the building. Still in excellent condition, it continues to serve as the county courthouse. Designated a National Historic Landmark in 1996.

# KANSAS

## HANOVER

**HOLLENBERG PONY EXPRESS STATION** The only unrestored station of the Pony Express still standing on its original site. The long, wooden building was the westernmost station of the Pony Express in Kansas. Mail carriers for the Pony Express rode on horseback for 35 to 75 miles (55 to 120 kilometers) before passing their pouches to fresh riders along the way. The Hollenberg facility was one of 190 home stations where such exchanges took place. (There were also many relay stations, where riders simply changed horses.) Famous for the spirit and daring of its carriers, the Pony Express operated for only 18 months—from April 1860 to October 1861.

The original Hollenberg Station was a small log cabin built in 1854 by a German immigrant and his wife, Gerat and Sophie Hollenberg. They sold supplies to travelers on the Oregon and California trails. Trade quickly increased, and the couple built the larger, five-room building that stands today. It is now a

### ❖ HANOVER ❖

🐾 A village located in northeastern Kansas, which is bordered by Nebraska, Missouri, Oklahoma, and Colorado

🐾 Located about 123 miles (198 kilometers) from the capital of Topeka

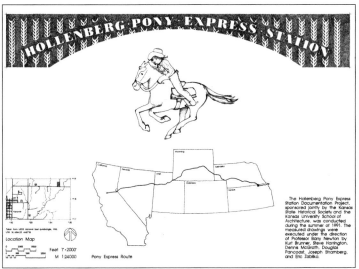

Location Map

Feet 1"-2000'

M 1:24000

Pony Express Route

The Hollenberg Pony Express Station Documentation Project, sponsored jointly by the Kansas State Historical Society and the Kansas University School of Architecture, was conducted during the summer of 1991. The measured drawings were executed under the direction of Professor Barry Newton by Kurt Brunner, Steve Harrington, Dennis McGrath, Douglas Pancoast, Joseph Stramberg, and Eric Zablika.

This map shows the historic route followed by most Pony Express riders—some of them only in their teens. They covered the present-day states of Kansas, Nebraska, Wyoming, Utah, Nevada, and California in just eight or nine days.

museum of pioneer life and the Pony Express. Designated a National Historic Landmark in 1961.

## LEAVENWORTH

**FORT LEAVENWORTH** United States Army post founded in 1827 by Colonel Henry Leavenworth to protect the Santa Fe Trail against Native Americans. Its strategic location in the heart of the frontier—overlooking the Missouri River in eastern Kansas—made it the chief base of operations in the Native American campaign for three decades. Fort Leavenworth also played a critical role in the Mexican War (1846–1848) and the Civil War (1861–1865), becoming the temporary capital of the Kansas Territory in 1854. In 1866, it became home to the Tenth Cavalry regiment, one of the first all-black units in the regular United

States Army—later known as the Buffalo Soldiers.

Fort Leavenworth has remained in continuous service since its founding. Today, it is a sprawling military complex with a number of operational and historic facilities. A military prison established there in 1874 continues to hold armed forces personnel convicted of serious offenses. The center of activity is the United States Army Command and General Staff College, an advanced officer training school founded in 1881. Its graduates have included such notable twentieth-century military leaders as generals Dwight D. Eisenhower, Omar Bradley, George Patton, Colin Powell, and Norman Schwarzkopf. Among the many historic attractions are the Frontier Army Museum, the Fort

### ❖ LEAVENWORTH ❖

- The oldest city in Kansas, settled in 1854 by proslavery Missourians
- A satellite community of Kansas City, located in northeastern Kansas on the Missouri River
- The site of the largest federal maximum security prison

Leavenworth National Cemetery, and a monument to the Buffalo Soldiers. Designated a National Historic Landmark in 1960.

---

MORE SITES

**CARRY A. NATION HOUSE** A small brick house in Medicine Lodge where the temperance, or antialcohol, crusader Carry Nation received a "divine call" to begin her hatchet-wielding campaign to wreck saloons. Today, it is a museum. Designated a National Historic Landmark in 1976.

### ★ PROFILE ★
### CARRY A. NATION

An agitator for prohibition—laws banning the sale and consumption of alcohol—at the turn of the twentieth century. Carry Amelia Bloomer Nation became widely feared by saloonkeepers for her violent campaign to destroy "drinking joints" and their stocks of liquor. She began her crusade in the 1890s after marrying an alcoholic. She also promoted the cause of temperance in lectures and pamphlets.

**COUNCIL GROVE HISTORIC DISTRICT** A stop on the Santa Fe Trail leading west. Council Grove's location at the edge of the Great Plains offered pioneers plentiful water, grass, and timber, and quickly became a supply center. The town includes several historic buildings and sites connected to the trail. Designated a National Historic Landmark in 1963.

# KENTUCKY

## DANVILLE

**JACOBS HALL, KENTUCKY SCHOOL FOR THE DEAF** The first publicly supported school for the deaf in the United States, established in 1823. Jacobs Hall, the oldest surviving building, was built between 1855 and 1857.

Efforts to fund, build, and staff the original institution were launched by two public officials, General Elias Barbee (whose daughter was deaf) and Judge John Rowan. Legislation authorizing the school was signed into law in December 1822. When it opened the following year, the Kentucky School for

Architect Major Thomas Lewinski designed Jacobs Hall (above) as well as Ashland, Henry Clay's home in Lexington, Kentucky.

the Deaf was also the first public institution of its kind west of the Allegheny Mountains.

Jacobs Hall, a four-story brick building in Italianate style, notable for its large roof brackets, housed the entire school from 1857 to 1882. At various times since, it has served as a classroom building, girls' dormitory, and teacher-staff residence. It is named for John Adamson Jacobs, the superintendent from 1835 to 1869. Today, it houses the superintendent's office and residence as well as a museum. The Kentucky School for the Deaf continues to prepare hearing-impaired students from preschool through high school for success in college, technical training, and vocational or professional employment. Designated a National Historic Landmark in 1965.

❖ DANVILLE ❖

- Established as the first capital of Kentucky in 1785

- A village located in the bluegrass region of southern Kentucky, which is bordered by Illinois, Indiana, Ohio, West Virginia, Virginia, Tennessee, and Missouri

- The "City of Firsts," Danville contains the West's first college (1783), political club (1786), and law school (1799); the first post office west of the Alleghenies (1792); and the nation's first African American kindergarten (1881).

HENRY CLAY HOME The estate, called Ashland, where one of America's most influential politicians of the pre–Civil War era lived for more than 40 years—1811 to 1852. A United States congressman and senator, secretary of state, and three-time candidate for president, Clay is best known for helping devise the Missouri Compromise of 1820. This plan tried to settle disputes over the extension of slavery into Western territories.

Clay and his wife, Lucretia, oversaw an estate that covered 600 acres (240 hectares) at its peak. With the help of the farm's enslaved people, they bred cattle and sheep and grew hemp, tobacco, and grains. The focal point of the property was the Ashland mansion, a magnificent two-story brick structure in the Federal style. Wings designed by Benjamin Latrobe, the leading American architect of the early nineteenth century, were added between 1813 and 1815.

Henry Clay's son, James Brown Clay, acquired Ashland after his father's death in 1852. Structural problems forced the younger Clay to tear down the house and rebuild it. The new structure was built on the original foundation, followed the same blueprint, and reused many of the original materials, but Italianate details were added. Work was completed in 1857. Much of the land was later sold, and Ashland was turned into a museum. Designated a National Historic Landmark in 1960.

- Named in 1775 by hunters camping there who heard news of the battle of Lexington, Massachusetts

- Located in central Kentucky in the heart of the bluegrass region

- Site of Mary Todd Lincoln's home and the Boone Station Historic Site

- A center for raising thoroughbred horses

## MORE SITES

**CHURCHILL DOWNS** The most famous horse racetrack in the United States, Churchill Downs in Louisville has been home to the Kentucky Derby since 1875. Modeled after Epsom Downs in England, it features a mile-long oval track and grandstands topped by spired cupolas, or domes. Designated a National Historic Landmark in 1986.

**LIBERTY HALL** Located in Frankfort, a two-story brick home built around 1800 by John Brown. A lawyer and political leader, Brown helped Kentucky achieve statehood in 1792. He also served as one of Kentucky's first senators. The home is built in the Federal style. The Brown family owned it until 1955. Today, it is open for guided tours. Designated a National Historic Landmark in 1971.

# LOUISIANA

## NEW ORLEANS

**DELTA QUEEN** Authentic Mississippi River steamboat, built in 1927. It is one of only two surviving steam-driven stern-wheel passenger boats—with rear paddlewheels. (The other is the *Belle of Louisville*.) Now a tourist attraction and overnight cruise boat, the 285-foot (87-meter) *Delta Queen* is a reminder of the major form of river transportation during the mid-1800s. With a shallow, flat-bottomed hull, the riverboat is designed for easy navigation through sandbars and shallows. It supports a multilevel, wood-and-steel superstructure with storage decks, elegant passenger quarters, and a pilothouse at the top. The golden age of

The Delta Queen can carry 174 passengers and 81 crew. The historic riverboat includes 87 staterooms, several restaurants and lounges, and a gift shop.

riverboating is vividly described by Mark Twain in *Life on the Mississippi* and other writings.

The *Delta Queen* originally steamed up and down the Sacramento River in CALIFORNIA. During World War II (1939–1945) it was used as a navy ferry in San Francisco Bay. After the war, it was towed through the Panama Canal to the mouth of the Mississippi River at New Orleans. Modern safety laws almost prevented its use in the mid-1960s, but public support led officials to grant special permission. A steam calliope on deck produces a loud whistle that announces the *Delta Queen* at its stops along the river. Designated a National Historic Landmark in 1989.

**THE FRENCH QUARTER** Also called the Vieux Carré (VIEW KA RAY) Historic District, French for "old square," the heart of New Orleans and the site of its original settlement in 1718. The rectangular district, located along the Mississippi River, was developed according to a plan drawn up in 1721. The unique cultural flavor of the French Quarter has made it one of the most popular tourist destinations in the United States.

The townhouses, churches, theaters, markets, and public squares of the French Quarter were built by Creole natives—descendants of French and Spanish settlers—in the eighteenth and early nineteenth centuries. The neighborhood went into decline after the Civil War (1861–1865). Starting in about 1940, however, the area began to be restored. Bourbon Street, now a world-famous entertainment strip, was the center of a thriving African American culture in the early 1900s that gave birth to modern jazz. St. Louis Cathedral on Jackson Square, built in 1794, is an architectural landmark. A statue of Andrew Jackson stands in the middle of the square, commemorating his victory over the British in 1815.

Creole and Cajun cooking, jazz clubs, and vintage buildings with wrought-iron balconies that overlook the streets contribute to the unique Old World atmosphere of the French Quarter. Mardi Gras, or "Fat Tuesday," celebrations attract throngs of revelers every winter. Designated a National Historic Landmark in 1965.

❖ **NEW ORLEANS** ❖

- Founded in 1718 by Jean Baptiste Le Moyne, sieur de Bienville, governor of the French colony of Louisiana
- Located on the Mississippi River in southeastern Louisiana, which is bordered by Texas, Arkansas, Mississippi, and the Gulf of Mexico
- Largest city in Louisiana and a major transportation and shipping hub
- Site of the nation's first movie theater, Vitascope Hall, which opened in 1896

MORE SITES

**HOMEPLACE PLANTATION HOUSE** A two-story cottage in French Colonial style, the Homeplace Plantation House was built between 1787 and 1791. Located in Hahnville, it is one of the oldest houses of the pre–Civil War era along the Mississippi River west of New Orleans. Designated a National Historic Landmark in 1970.

**THE CABILDO** A large building on historic Jackson Square next to the cathedral in New Orleans, the Cabildo was erected between 1795 and 1799 to house the Spanish colonial council, or *cabildo*. After the Louisiana Purchase in 1803, it served as city hall, the state Supreme Court, and, since 1911, the Louisiana State Museum. Designated a National Historic Landmark in 1960.

The French Quarter is a favorite attraction for visitors, offering carriage rides, restaurants, coffee shops, and souvenir stands.

# MAINE

BRUNSWICK

**HARRIET BEECHER STOWE HOUSE**
The home of the author Harriet Beecher Stowe from 1850 to 1852. Stowe wrote her most famous novel, *Uncle Tom's Cabin*, while she lived in this two-and-a-half story frame house.

Published in 1852, *Uncle Tom's Cabin* describes the physical and emotional abuse that enslaved people endured. The book became a bestseller and was translated into more than 60 languages. It stirred up antislavery feelings in the North as it exposed the horrors of slavery. Although Stowe had never visited the

### ❖ BRUNSWICK ❖

- First European settlers came to the area in the 1630s
- Founded as a town in 1739
- Located on the Atlantic coast of Maine, which is bordered by New Hampshire, the Atlantic Ocean, and the Canadian provinces of Quebec and New Brunswick
- A town about 27 miles (43.4 kilometers) north of Portland
- An early shipbuilding center, nearly 100 vessels were built in Brunswick between 1789 and 1807
- In the second half of the nineteenth century, immigrants from Quebec filled the need for Brunswick's mill workers.

South, she wrote her emotion-filled novel based on her own moving experiences in Cincinnati, OHIO, and on firsthand stories of the conditions of enslaved people.

The impact of the book was widespread. According to legend, upon meeting Stowe in 1862, President Lincoln remarked, "So you're the little woman who wrote the book that started this Great War!" Designated a National Historic Landmark in 1962.

★ PROFILE ★

## HARRIET BEECHER STOWE

An American abolitionist and writer whose famous novel, *Uncle Tom's Cabin*, helped stir antislavery feelings in the North in the years before the Civil War (1861–1865).

Harriet Beecher was born in Litchfield, CONNECTICUT, in 1811. Her father, a minister and an abolitionist, greatly influenced young Harriet and her ten brothers and sisters. In 1832, the Beecher family moved to Cincinnati, OHIO, located across the river from the slave state of KENTUCKY. In Cincinnati, Harriet learned firsthand the horrors of slavery. She married Professor Calvin E. Stowe in 1836. The Stowes were deeply affected by the cruel conditions of slavery and helped runaways on the Underground Railroad.

In 1850, the family moved to Brunswick, Maine, where Calvin Stowe had joined the faculty of Bowdoin College. Harriet Beecher Stowe wrote *Uncle Tom's Cabin* while living in Brunswick. *See also* ILLINOIS, VERMONT.

## ROCKLAND HARBOR

***LEWIS R. FRENCH*** Completed in 1871, the only surviving coasting schooner of thousands that were built and the oldest known sailing vessel in Maine. The *Lewis R. French* carried many different types of cargo, including lumber, bricks, granite, and lime. The ship was first a sailing vessel, but later a motor was added. The *Lewis R. French* was completely restored in 1976 and today serves as a Maine windjammer. Just as the crew did more than 100 years ago, people from all over the country travel to Maine to sail on the *French*. Designated a National Historic Landmark in 1992.

In 1992, the *Louis R. French* left its homeport in Maine and sailed to Boston, Massachussetts, to celebrate the five hundredth anniversary of Christopher Columbus's voyage to America.

## ❖ ROCKLAND HARBOR ❖

🐾 Part of the rocky Atlantic coast of Maine, about 43 miles (69 kilometers) east of Augusta, the state capital

🐾 The Shore Village Museum boasts the largest collection of lighthouse memorabilia in the United States.

## MORE SITES

**WINSLOW HOMER STUDIO** The carriage house located in the small town of Scarborough, where the famous artist painted from 1884 until his death in 1910. Although Homer painted landscapes and Civil War scenes, he is perhaps most famous for his striking images of the sea. Designated a National Historic Landmark in 1965.

**JAMES G. BLAINE HOUSE** Located in Augusta, the home of Republican politician James G. Blaine for more than 30 years. Blaine served as Speaker of the House of Representatives, a U.S. senator, and secretary of state. He ran unsuccessfully for president in 1884. The state acquired the large frame house in 1919, renovated it, and made it the governor's mansion. Today, it still serves as the governor's house and is open to the public for tours. Designated a National Historic Landmark in 1964.

# MARYLAND

ANNAPOLIS

**COLONIAL ANNAPOLIS HISTORIC DISTRICT** The "old city" of Maryland's capital, located on the Severn River near Chesapeake Bay. Lined with vintage pre-Revolutionary buildings, its picturesque streets attract many visitors. Annapolis was named for England's Princess (later Queen) Anne in 1694, when it became the capital of colonial Maryland. The city served as a temporary national capital from November 1783 to August 1784, during which time it hosted the Continental Congress.

First settled in 1649, the town was laid out by Sir Francis Nicholson, the colonial governor, in 1694. Narrow streets radiate out from central circles like spokes from hubs. At the center of the downtown area stands the Maryland Capitol, the oldest statehouse still in use in the United States. It was in this building that General George Washington resigned as commander of

## ❖ ANNAPOLIS ❖

🐾 Founded as Providence in 1649 by English settlers

🐾 Located on the Severn River in central Maryland, which is bordered by Pennsylvania, Delaware, Virginia, West Virginia, and the Atlantic Ocean

🐾 Later known as Anne Arundel Town, after the Second Lord Baltimore's wife, but renamed Annapolis for England's Princess Anne

The boundaries of the Annapolis Historic District are almost the same as Annapolis's 1695 borders. Today, the area is a vibrant part of the city and a favorite stop for tourists.

the Continental Army in December 1783. Weeks later, in January 1784, Congress convened there to ratify the Treaty of Paris, ending the Revolutionary War. Other attractions include St. John's College; many houses and churches dating to the eighteenth century; and a variety of museums, galleries, and shops. It is also home to the United States Naval Academy. Designated a National Historic Landmark in 1965.

## BALTIMORE

**FORT MCHENRY** United States military installation on Whetstone Point in Baltimore harbor and site of a battle during the

War of 1812 that inspired Francis Scott Key to write the words of "The Star-Spangled Banner." On September 13, 1814, British ships began bombarding the fort to protect ground troops attempting to land and take the city. The attack continued through the night. When Key saw the American flag still flying over Fort McHenry the next morning, he was moved to write his verse. The garrison stayed in American hands, and the enemy withdrew.

Fort McHenry was built in 1799 and named for James McHenry, who served

### ★ PROFILE ★
### FRANCIS SCOTT KEY

A Maryland-born lawyer and poet, Francis Scott Key (1779–1843) is famous for writing the lyrics of "The Star-Spangled Banner" after a night-long attack on Fort McHenry during the War of 1812. Put to an old English melody, the song was officially adopted as the national anthem in 1931. Key maintained a private law practice in WASHINGTON, D.C., and served as a U.S. attorney from 1833 to 1841. His other verses and songs were published in *Poems of the Late Francis S. Key* (1857).

as United States secretary of war from 1794 to 1800. It was used for various purposes after the War of 1812, including a storage depot and military prison. The 43-acre (17-hectare) battle site was designated as a national park in 1925. Its status was changed to national monument and historic shrine in 1939.

---

## MORE SITES

**CLARA BARTON HOUSE** A large frame house in Glen Echo where the famous battlefield nurse and founder of the American Red Cross lived from 1897 to her death in 1912. It was also Red Cross headquarters until 1904. Designated a National Landmark in 1965.

**RACHEL CARSON HOUSE** A ranch-style brick house in Silver Spring where the noted biologist and author lived from 1956 until her death in 1964. It was here that Carson wrote *Silent Spring* (1962), a groundbreaking work of the environmental movement. Deisgnated a National Historic Landmark in 1991.

---

# MASSACHUSETTS

### BOSTON

**BOSTON COMMON** Located near the center of Boston, one of the oldest public parks in the United States. The term *com-*

❖ **B O S T O N** ❖

- First settled by Puritans from England in 1630
- State capital of Massachusetts, which is bordered by Rhode Island, Connecticut, New York, Vermont, New Hampshire, and the Atlantic Ocean
- The city of Boston has had three names: the Algonquin Indians called it Shawmut; then the Puritans named it Trimountain, after the three peaks on Beacon Hill. The Puritans eventually chose Boston because many of them were from an English town of the same name.

*mon* refers to the fact that the land was set aside for the public's use. It covers almost 50 acres (20.2 hectares) and was set aside in 1634 as a cow pasture and a training area for the city's militia. Just before the outbreak of the American Revolution in 1775, British troops camped in the park. Cows continued to graze on the Common until 1834. Today, in nice weather, the Common is filled with tourists and people relaxing. The Common is also where protesters, expressing their right of free speech, often gather. Designated a National Historic Landmark in 1987.

**OLD NORTH CHURCH** Completed in 1740, Boston's second Anglican Church. Its official name is Christ Church. It was made famous in a poem by Henry Wadsworth Longfellow. The poem, "Paul

Reverend Timothy Cutler held the first service in Christ Church—often called Old North Church—on December 29, 1723, years before the building was finished.

The steeple is 191 feet (58.2 meters) tall, making it the highest in Boston. Inside the church are box pews with high sides, arranged in an orderly grid pattern. During the cold colonial winters, church members brought metal boxes with hot coals inside to warm their feet. The metal boxes, combined with the high sides of the pews, helped church members keep warm in the drafty, unheated church.

The two lanterns hung in its steeple, signaling the arrival of the British by sea, on the night of April 18, 1775, made Old North Church an important part of the American Revolution. Seeing the two lanterns, Paul Revere rode toward Lexington, a town about 11 miles (17.7 kilometers) inland, warning the colonists that British troops were sailing up the Charles River. The British planned to

Revere's Ride," describes the midnight journey of Revere, who rode to warn the American colonists about the coming British troops.

HISTORY Designed by the print dealer William Price, Christ Church took 17 years to be built—from 1723 to 1740. A fine example of colonial Georgian architecture, the church is built of reddish brick, but its steeple is made of wood.

★ PROFILE ★
PAUL REVERE

An American patriot and craftsman, Paul Revere is best remembered for his famous midnight ride, warning the Boston countryside of the advancing British troops. Revere was also a leading Boston silversmith, engraver, and businessman. A well-known engraving created by Revere of the 1770 Boston Massacre stirred up colonial feelings against the British. He continued his anti-British activities throughout the 1770s. He was probably among the colonists who disguised themselves as Native Americans, boarded a British ship, and threw 342 chests of tea into Boston Harbor in 1773—an event known as the Boston Tea Party.

seize the colonists' gunpowder hidden in Concord, a town near Lexington. The colonial militia marched to Lexington to meet the British troops. In the early morning hours of April 19, 1775, British and American troops clashed, firing the first shots of the American Revolution.

TODAY The two lanterns that signaled Paul Revere are remembered with a parade and an annual reenactment of Revere's ride. Two lanterns are carried up to the steeple, and Paul Revere once again dashes away on horseback. Still an active Episcopal church, it is open every day for visiting and prayer. Designated a National Historic Landmark in 1961.

In July 2000, the USS *Constitution* led a parade of tall ships into Boston Harbor to celebrate the millennium—a rare trip for the nation's oldest warship.

**USS CONSTITUTION** Launched in 1797, the oldest warship in the world. Throughout its long history, the USS *Constitution* engaged in about 40 battles without a loss. During the War of 1812, the ship earned the nickname "Old Ironsides" after British cannonballs bounced off its sides. During the 1800s, the *Constitution* served around the world, including in the Pacific, off the Atlantic coast of Africa, and in the Mediterranean Sea. In 1855, it became a training ship for sailors. Because of the ship's legendary fame, it was restored and turned into a museum in the 1920s. Although Boston became the *Constitution*'s official homeport in 1954, it still sails on special occasions. Today, the ship—more than two hundred years old—is open to the public in the Charleston Navy Yard. Designated a National Historic Landmark in 1960.

## CONCORD

**WALDEN POND** Located about one-and-a-half miles south of the town of Concord, a rural site where the writer Henry David Thoreau lived from 1845 to 1847. He built a one-room cabin on the shore of the 100-foot (30.4-meter) deep pond where he reflected on his life while surrounded by natural beauty and clear water. Here, he penned his most famous work, *Walden*. This classic essay, published in 1854, describes the environment and the beauty of nature. In 1922, the owners gave the area to the state of Massachusetts to keep it from becoming commercialized. They asked that Walden be preserved as a park, much as it was in Thoreau's time. Today, to protect the pond's fragile environment, only 1,000 visitors may enter the park at a time. Designated a National Historic Landmark in 1962.

### ❖ CONCORD ❖

- First settled by the English in 1635
- Site of the second battle of the American Revolution
- Paul Revere never reached Concord to warn the colonists, but Dr. John Prescott did.

## LEXINGTON

**LEXINGTON GREEN** Site of the American Revolution's first battle, fought in the early morning hours of April 19, 1775. The battle marked a turning point in the relations between Great Britain and the American colonies. The battle began with the famous "shot heard 'round the world" immortalized in Ralph Waldo Emerson's "Concord Hymn."

HISTORY Relations between Britain and the colonies became strained at the end of the French and Indian War in 1763.

After the war, Britain was in debt and tried to raise money by taxing the colonists. Believing their rights as British citizens were being ignored by the king, the colonists' protests grew more intense. Such events as the Boston Massacre and the Boston Tea Party increased the tension. By February 1775, King George III had declared the colony of Massachusetts to be in rebellion, and hundreds of British troops, under the command of General Thomas Gage, were stationed in Boston. The colonists then formed an army of American citizens known as the "Minute Men" because they vowed to be ready at a minute's notice.

Hearing that the colonists had stored a large supply of gunpowder in Concord, a town a few miles outside of Boston, General Gage ordered his troops to seize the illegal powder. The patriot Paul Revere rode to warn the Minute Men of the coming British troops. At Lexington Green, about 70 Minute Men faced about 1,000 British soldiers. No one knows who fired the first shot. When the smoke

### ❖ LEXINGTON ❖

- First settled by the English in 1642
- Site of the first shots of the American Revolution
- Site of America's first Revolutionary War monument, an obelisk (or four-sided pillar), in Lexington Green

cleared, eight colonists lay dead and ten were wounded.

The British then marched to Concord but found that the colonists had removed most of the gunpowder. As they retreated to Boston, angry colonists fired upon the British troops from behind trees and stone walls, a battle resulting in about 250 British casualties.

TODAY Lexington Green is still a public park. Among the many memorials on the Green is the famous statue *Lexington Minute Man*. Every year, a reenactment of the battle is held on the third Monday in April—Patriot's Day. Designated a National Historic Landmark in 1961.

## WESTPORT

**PAUL CUFFE FARM** The home purchased in 1797 by Paul Cuffe, a free African American merchant and sea captain. Cuffe's businesses made him wealthy, enabling him to become a leading citizen in his community of Westport. He fought discrimination and, through his work, won African Americans in Massachusetts the right to vote in 1783. Sailing to Africa in 1815, he helped start a colony of free African Americans, which later grew into the country of Liberia. Cuffe died in 1817 and is buried in Westport. The farm is still privately owned. Designated a National Historic Landmark in 1974.

## ❖ WESTPORT ❖

- First settled by the English in 1670
- Westport Point originally was used by the Wampanoag Indians as a summer encampment, called "Pacquachuck" or "cleared hill."
- Purchased from the Indians in 1652 by the elders of the Plymouth colony, then sold in parts to Quakers and Baptists escaping religious persecution
- Once a major port of the whaling industry and now a tourist haven

## MORE SITES

**HANCOCK SHAKER VILLAGE** Located in the Berkshire Hills of western Massachusetts—about 5 miles (8 kilometers) south of Pittsfield—a Shaker religious community from 1793 to 1960. The village is now an outdoor history museum where Shaker life and artifacts can be studied. Designated a National Historic Landmark in 1968.

**LONGFELLOW HOUSE** Home of the famous poet Henry Wadsworth Longfellow from 1837 to 1882. Built in Cambridge (5 miles [8 kilometers] outside of Boston proper) in 1759 for John Vassal. A British loyalist, Vassal left the house as the American Revolution approached. The Georgian-style home served as George Washington's army headquarters at the beginning of the Revolution. Today, it is a museum. Designated a National Historic Landmark in 1972.

# MICHIGAN

## DETROIT

**GENERAL MOTORS BUILDING** Former headquarters of the largest automobile manufacturer in the world. Occupying a full city block in downtown Detroit, the building was completed in 1923. The American architect Albert Kahn, best known for his innovative automobile assembly plants, designed it. Made of steel-frame construction with limestone facing, the main building features four 15-story wings atop a central block and connecting "spine." A five-story annex is attached. A "city within a city," the building has 30 acres (12 hectares) of floor space, with 1,800 offices, shops, and restaurants, an auditorium, a gymnasium, and other facilities. The company moved to new headquarters in the 1990s and donated the building to the city. Designated a National Historic Landmark in 1978.

## MACKINAC ISLAND

**MACKINAC ISLAND** Once the military and fur-trading center of the Great Lakes region, now a popular summer resort. Located in the Straits of Mackinac (between the northern and southern peninsulas of Michigan), the heavily wooded island is only 6 square miles (16 square kilometers) in area. Its largest and most visited site is Old Fort Mackinac, begun by the British in 1780 and completed by Americans in 1800. Mackinac Island became a summer resort in the late nineteenth century. One of the island's most famous hotels, the

The Victorian-style Grand Hotel on Mackinac Island was completed in 1887. Its 381 rooms offer guests many luxuries, including several restaurants and lounges.

🪰 Founded in the early 1800s as a center of trade with Native Americans

🪰 A village on the south end of Mackinac Island, which is located in a channel between two Great Lakes—Lake Huron and Lake Michigan

🪰 The main means of transportation are bicycle, horseback, and carriage. The village does not allow motor vehicles and is accessible only by air in winter.

Grand Hotel, is a wooden structure with a porch 628 feet (191.4 meters) long. In 1875, it became the second national park in the United States. The island was transferred to the state of Michigan in 1895 and became Michigan's first state park. No cars are allowed. Designated a National Historic Landmark in 1960.

## MORE SITES

**HENRY FORD MUSEUM AND GREEN-FIELD VILLAGE** An indoor/outdoor history museum in Dearborn dedicated to the life and vision of the automobile manufacturer Henry Ford. The museum itself, nicknamed "Henry's Attic," collects his personal memorabilia and a vast number of other artifacts. Greenfield Village brings together original buildings from the family homestead, Ford's early workshops and factories, buildings from other places, special exhibits, shops, and restaurants. Also included are the Wright Brothers' workshop from Dayton, OHIO, and the bus Rosa Parks

rode in from Montgomery, ALABAMA. Designated a National Historic Landmark in 1981.

**MICHIGAN STATE CAPITOL** Located in Lansing, one of the first state capitols to be modeled after the United States Capitol in WASHINGTON, D.C. Built between 1872 and 1876, it was designed by Elijah E. Myers, a well-known architect of the time. The interior of the building is famous for its ornate Victorian style and was restored in the 1990s. Designated a National Historic Landmark in 1992. *See also* GEORGIA.

# MINNESOTA

## ROCHESTER

**MAYO CLINIC BUILDINGS** An innovative and still famous medical center established by the brothers William J. and Charles H. Mayo in the 1890s and 1900s. The Rochester clinic was the first private group practice in which medical specialists and researchers cooperated in the

🪰 Settled in the 1850s as a crossroads camp for wagon trains

🪰 Located in southeastern Minnesota, which is bordered by Wisconsin, Iowa, South Dakota, North Dakota, the Canadian provinces of Manitoba and Ontario, and Lake Superior

🪰 Named after Rochester, New York, by a settler from there

More than 6 million people have been treated at the Mayo Clinic since its founding. Today, the Mayo Foundation includes three clinics and four hospitals in three states.

treatment of patients. The original main building (1914), the first complete clinic in the United States, was demolished in 1986. The historic Plummer Building (1926–1928) still stands. The Rochester complex today includes two large hospitals, St. Mary's and Rochester Methodist. Together they have more than 1,800 beds and employ 1,100 physicians and scientists. The Mayo Foundation also operates major clinics in Jacksonville, FLORIDA, and Scottsdale, ARIZONA. It was designated a National Historic Landmark in 1969.

**F. SCOTT FITZGERALD HOUSE** A Victorian stone row house at 599 Summit Avenue, where the novelist and short-story writer lived from July 1919 to early 1920 while completing his first novel, *This Side of Paradise*. The 23-year-old Fitzgerald moved back to his parents' home after attending Princeton, serving in the Army, and then leaving a New York City advertising job. Working in a quiet upstairs room, he revised the manuscript, originally titled *The Romantic Egoist*, which made him famous. He went on to become one of America's greatest twentieth-century authors. The Summit Terrace row houses, then an exclusive St. Paul address, remain relatively unchanged today. Designated a National Historic Landmark in 1971.

❖ **ST. PAUL** ❖

- Founded as "Pig's Eye" in 1838, after the first settler, Pierre "Pig's Eye" Parrant; renamed for St. Paul Church, built in 1841
- State capital of Minnesota
- St. Paul and Minneapolis form the Twin Cities metropolitan area.

MORE SITES

**CHARLES A. LINDBERGH, SR., HOUSE** From 1907 to 1920, the Morrison County home of political leader Charles A. Lindbergh, Sr., and his son, later to become a world-renowned aviator. Lindbergh, Sr. was a prominent U.S. congressman (1907–1917). Charles A. Lindbergh, Jr., became the first person to fly solo across the Atlantic Ocean in May 1927. Designated a National Historic Landmark in 1976.

**MOUNTAIN IRON MINE** A large iron mine, discovered in 1890, which produced more than half of all the iron ore in the country. Located in the Mesabi Range, the mine closed in 1956 and was filled with water soon after. Today, it is a reservoir. Designated a National Historic Landmark in 1968.

# MISSISSIPPI

## NATCHEZ

**STANTON HALL** Among the grandest of the many pre–Civil War Southern mansions in this old Mississippi River port city. Built between 1851 and 1857 for Frederick Stanton, a wealthy cotton broker, the house occupies a full square block atop a downtown hillside. Magnificent in size and rich in design, it is fronted by a large portico, or porch, with four giant Corinthian columns. Interior moldings, marble mantelpieces, gold-frame mirrors, bronze chandeliers, and other appointments were imported from Europe in a specially chartered ship. Always a showplace, Stanton Hall has been restored as a museum. Designated a National Historic Landmark in 1974.

## ❖ NATCHEZ ❖

- ❧ Founded in 1716, when Fort Rosalie was established
- ❧ Located in southwest Mississippi, which is bordered by Arkansas, Tennessee, Alabama, Louisiana, and the Gulf of Mexico
- ❧ Served as capital of Mississippi Territory (1798–1802) and state capital (1817–1821)
- ❧ One of the oldest towns on the Mississippi River and a cultural and trade center for wealthy plantation owners before the Civil War (1861–1865)

## OXFORD

**WILLIAM FAULKNER HOUSE** A two-story Greek Revival frame house where the great Southern novelist and short-story writer lived from 1930 until his death in 1962. Faulkner wrote most of the novels and stories that earned him

## ❖ OXFORD ❖

- ❧ Settled in the 1830s by pioneers from Virginia and the Carolinas on lands once held by the Chickasaw
- ❧ Located in northern Mississippi
- ❧ Site of Mississippi's first university, Oxford is named after the university town in England.
- ❧ Burned by Union forces in 1864, Oxford still contains fine pre–Civil War houses that are the center of its tourist economy.

The William Faulkner House reopened in spring 2003 after undergoing renovations, including the addition of a new air-conditioning system designed to maintain a constant temperature and humidity inside the house.

his reputation—and the Nobel Prize for Literature—during his years there. The people and places of his fictional Yoknapatawpha County, the setting for many of his major works, are based on life in and around Oxford. A local planter built the house, which he called Rowan Oak, in about 1840. Today, it is the property of the University of Mississippi, which maintains it as a museum and library. Designated a National Historic Landmark in 1968.

## MORE SITES

**SIEGE AND BATTLE OF CORINTH SITES** The northern Mississippi location of a Union siege in the spring of 1862 that forced Confederate troops to evacuate a major railroad hub. In early October of that year, Union forces held off a Southern attack in the Battle of Corinth. Designated a National Historic Landmark in 1991.

**ROSALIE** Located in Natchez, a large pre–Civil War mansion built for a wealthy cotton seller in 1823. The front of the house includes a large portico, or open porch, in the Tuscan style. Union forces occupied the mansion and used it as their headquarters after the 1863 Confederate surrender of Vicksburg, Mississippi. Today, it is a museum. Designated a National Historic Landmark in 1989.

# MISSOURI

## HANNIBAL

**MARK TWAIN BOYHOOD HOME** A white, two-story frame house that was home to Samuel Langhorne Clemens

### ❖ HANNIBAL ❖

- Founded by Moses Bates in 1819
- Located on the Mississippi River in northeast Missouri, which is bordered by Iowa, Illinois, Kentucky, Tennessee, Arkansas, Oklahoma, Kansas, and Nebraska
- An east-west crossroads greatly influenced by the California gold rush of 1849

The writer, lecturer, and humorist Mark Twain (pen name of Samuel Langhorne Clemens, 1835–1910) was enormously popular during his lifetime and earned a place among the giants of American literature. In addition to *The Adventures of Tom Sawyer* (1876), *The Adventures of Huckleberry Finn* (1884), and other classic tales, he wrote comic sketches, travel pieces, and essays that are still widely read and loved today.

(Mark Twain's real name) from 1844, when he was nine, to 1853, when he left Hannibal. His boyhood experiences in the Mississippi River town provided the raw material for his most beloved works, especially *The Adventures of Tom Sawyer* (1876) and *The Adventures of Huckleberry Finn* (1884).

John Marshall Clemens, Sam's father, built the house in 1844. The original dwelling had only three rooms on one floor. In 1851, Sam's older brother, Orion, began using the parlor as the publishing offices and printing room for his newspaper, the *Hannibal Journal*. A second floor was added to increase living space. With the exception of a small museum built next door in 1935, the property remains largely unchanged from the days of Mark Twain's youth. Along a sidewalk at the side of the house stands a white picket fence like the one Tom Sawyer tricked his friends into painting. Desig-

nated a National Historic Landmark in 1962. *See also* CONNECTICUT, LOUISIANA, and NEVADA.

## ST. LOUIS

**GATEWAY ARCH** The tallest monument in the United States and symbol of the city's status as "Gateway to the West." The gleaming stainless-steel structure stands 630 feet (192 meters) above downtown St. Louis on the west bank of the Mississippi River. The Finnish-American architect Eero

The Gateway Arch in St. Louis cost $13 million to build—$11 million for the arch itself and $2 million for the arch transportation system.

Saarinen designed the arch in 1947. Groundbreaking began in 1959, and a formal dedication took place on May 25, 1968.

The design was chosen out of hundreds of entries in a competition for an appropriate monument at the Jefferson National Expansion Memorial—the park in which it now stands. President Franklin D. Roosevelt had established that national historic site in 1935 to honor Thomas Jefferson and others responsible for the expansion of U.S. territory in the nineteenth century.

The Gateway Arch takes the form of an inverted catenary—a chain or cord hung between two fixed points. It was constructed by welding together large, double-walled triangular sections, like links in a chain. On the lower half of both legs, the spaces between the double walls are filled with concrete. Visitors can ride to the top of the arch in small cars that travel inside the two legs. An observation room at the peak provides spectacular views of Missouri to the west and ILLINOIS to the east. Designated a National Historic Landmark in 1987.

❖ ST. LOUIS ❖

🌿 Settled in 1764 as a French fur-trading post

🌿 Located in eastern Missouri below the mouth of the Missouri River

🌿 Named after King Louis IX of France

🌿 The largest city in Missouri and the nation's second largest inland river port

MORE SITES

**MISSOURI BOTANICAL GARDENS**
One of the oldest botanical gardens in the United States, founded in 1859 by Henry Shaw. Today, the popular St. Louis attraction is also among the world's leading botanical research centers. Designated a National Historic Landmark in 1976.

**WESTMINSTER COLLEGE GYMNASIUM**
Located in Fulton, Missouri, site of a famous speech by former British Prime Minister Winston Churchill on March 5, 1946. His statement that "an iron curtain has descended" across Europe coined a phrase that described East-West tensions for decades to come. Designated a National Historic Landmark in 1968.

# MONTANA

GLACIER NATIONAL PARK

**GOING-TO-THE-SUN ROAD** A scenic, two-lane highway that crosses Glacier National Park from east to west. A marvel of engineering and natural beauty, the 52-mile (84-kilometer) road was built by the Bureau of Public Roads and the National Park Service between 1921 and 1932. Considered one of the world's most spectacular scenic drives—through deep gorges, open tundra, cedar forests, and

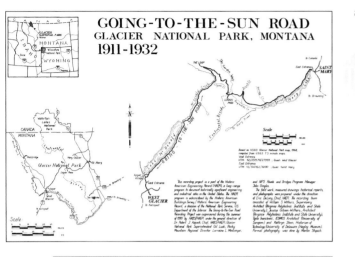

A map from 1932 shows the location of Going-to-the-Sun Road, an engineering marvel in northern Montana.

glacial terrain—the road follows the natural contours of the landscape to make previously inaccessible areas available to motorists. Because of the long, harsh winters in northern Montana, most of the highway is open only from early June to mid-October. Only cars are allowed. Designated a National Historic Landmark in 1997.

## ❖ GLACIER NATIONAL PARK ❖

- 🌿 Preserves more than 1 million acres (404,678 hectares) of forests, meadows, and lakes

- 🌿 Home to about 70 species of mammals and 260 species of birds

- 🌿 Recent studies show evidence of humans from more than 10,000 years ago

- 🌿 French, Spanish, and English trappers were the first Europeans to visit the area.

**RANKIN RANCH** The summer home from 1923 to 1956 of Jeannette Rankin, the first female member of the United States House of Representatives (1917–1919 and 1941–1943). The frame house, which belonged to her brother, had been the main building on a 3-square-mile (7.8-square-kilometer) cattle ranch. Rankin, who was born and raised on a ranch outside Missoula, Montana, took joy in the open spaces of Broadwater County east of Helena. For more than 30 years of her life as a politician, peace advocate, and feminist, she spent almost every summer at the ranch. Designated a National Historic Landmark in 1976.

## ★ PROFILE ★
## JEANETTE RANKIN

The first woman to serve in the United States Congress, Rankin (1880–1973) was twice elected as a Republican from Montana, in 1916 and 1940. A lifelong pacifist, or peace advocate, she was the only member of Congress to vote against America's entry into both World War I (1914–1918) and World War II (1939–1945). In the late 1960s, she was an outspoken opponent of American involvement in the Vietnam War (1964–1975). Rankin was also an active feminist, working on behalf of suffrage and women's rights.

- Founded in 1864 after the discovery of gold in Last Chance Gulch
- Located in the Rocky Mountains in west-central Montana
- State capital of Montana, which is bordered by North Dakota, South Dakota, Wyoming, Idaho, and the Canadian provinces of British Columbia, Alberta, and Saskatchewan
- Gold and silver lured miners to the area, but as those supplies became exhausted, the miners turned to copper, lead, and zinc.

## MORE SITES

### BANNACK HISTORIC DISTRICT
Now preserved as a ghost town, the site of a major gold strike on Willards (now Grasshopper) Creek in July 1862. Springing up almost overnight, Bannack became capital of the newly established Montana Territory in 1864. Designated a National Historic Landmark in 1961.

### CHARLES M. RUSSELL HOUSE A
frame house in Great Falls where the popular Western artist and sculptor lived from 1900 to 1926. A log studio he built in 1903 now houses a museum. Designated a National Historic Landmark in 1965.

# NEBRASKA

## BOYS TOWN

### FATHER FLANAGAN'S BOYS' HOME
A community established outside Omaha in 1921 that provides care and education for homeless, delinquent, abused, and handicapped children. Father Flanagan began the program in 1917 with five boys at an old rented house in downtown Omaha. Four years later, with the help of public contributions, he moved the home to spacious Overlook Farm outside the city. Later expanded to 1,300 acres (525 hectares), the Boys Town community was incorporated as a village in 1936. The 1938 motion picture *Boys Town*, starring Spencer Tracy and Mickey Rooney, made the institution familiar to millions of Americans. Girls were accepted in 1979.

Boys Town has pioneered juvenile care by providing a family-style environment, an atmosphere of shared responsibility, regular education, health facilities, and close adult supervision. Today, the Omaha Boys Town is home to some five hundred children of mixed age and background. The village has its own post office, police, firehouse, and clinic. Boys Town also runs programs in several other states and foreign countries. Designated a National Historic Landmark in 1985.

Father Flanagan, Boys Town's founder, saw a drawing of the two brothers in a magazine and contacted the magazine for permission to use the image as a symbol of Boys Town. Permission was granted and a statue was commissioned. The original is now in the Girls and Boys Center in the Village of Boys Town.

## RED CLOUD

**WILLA CATHER HOUSE** Childhood home of fiction writer and journalist Willa Cather (1873–1974), from the age of 10 to 17. Although she moved east as a young woman, she drew on her youthful experiences in Nebraska to write acclaimed novels of the pioneer experience. Such works as *O Pioneers!* (1913), *My Ántonia* (1918), and *A Lost Lady* (1923) describe the spirit and traditions of life on the prairie. Six of Cather's 12 novels and a number of her short stories are set in Red Cloud and surrounding Webster County.

In her novel *The Song of the Lark* (1915), Cather lovingly describes a one-and-a-half-story white frame house like the one in Red Cloud. From 1884 to 1890, which she later called her "formative years," she occupied a small attic bedroom with a slanted ceiling and rose-colored wallpaper, which she hung herself. Today, the

★ PROFILE ★
## FATHER EDWARD JOSEPH FLANAGAN

**A** Roman Catholic priest who moved from his native Ireland to the United States at age 18, Father Flanagan (1886–1948) is known as the founder of Boys Town. After being ordained as a priest in the Omaha diocese in 1912, he began working with homeless and jobless men. He then turned his attention to the plight of abused, neglected, and abandoned boys. Believing that "there is no such thing as a bad boy," Father Flanagan became known as an authority on juvenile delinquency. After World War II (1939–1945), he worked to set up youth projects in Korea and Japan.

🌾 Incorporated in 1872

🌾 Located on the Republican River in southern Nebraska

🌾 Named for a famous Native American chief from the Sioux tribe

🌾 First city in Nebraska to elect a woman mayor, Mary Peterson (1921–1927)

🌾 The mainstays of the local economy are grain, dairy, and poultry products.

house is a museum dedicated to Cather and her work. It contains several family artifacts, and many details remain unchanged from her childhood—including the rose-colored wallpaper. Designated a National Historic Landmark in 1971.

## MORE SITES

**FAIRVIEW** A Victorian brick house on a farm outside Lincoln, Nebraska, that was the residence of political leader William Jennings Bryan from 1902 to 1921. An inspirational orator, Bryan (1860–1925) held public receptions and political rallies at his home. He was a two-term U.S. congressman, secretary of state, and Democratic nominee for president in 1896, 1900, and 1908. He lost all three times. Designated a National Historic Landmark in 1963.

**NEBRASKA STATE CAPITOL** Located in Lincoln, one of the most distinctive state capitols in the nation. Designed by

architect Bertram Grosvenor Goodhue, the Moderne style building took ten years to complete, from 1922 to 1932, and cost less than $10 million. A 400-foot (121.9-meter) domed tower looms over the building. On top of the dome is *The Sower*, a 19-foot (5.79-meter) sculpture symbolizing the state's farming heritage. Designated a National Historic Landmark in 1976.

# NEVADA

## BOULDER CITY

**HOOVER DAM** A giant concrete dam on the lower Colorado River between Nevada and ARIZONA. A major feat of engineering, Hoover Dam was the world's largest when the last concrete was poured (1935). It is a multipurpose gravity-arch dam. (Its great height and curved shape enable it to withstand the enormous pressure of the water it holds back.) Hoover Dam rises 726 feet (221 meters) above the Colorado River and measures 1,244 feet (379 meters) across the top. Its backup water created the Lake Mead reservoir. The massive

🌾 Once Nevada's largest city

🌾 During the construction of Hoover Dam, the population swelled to more than 7,000.

🌾 Incorporated as a city in 1958

structure contains an amazing 3.25 million cubic yards (2.49 million cubic meters) of concrete.

Construction of the Hoover Dam began in 1931 and took five years to complete. Although the concrete was completed in 1935, other work continued until March 1, 1936. It was originally called Boulder Dam, but Congress renamed it in honor of former President Herbert Hoover in 1947. In addition to flood control, the dam provides hydroelectric power, irrigation, and drinking water for areas throughout the Southwest and as far away as CALIFORNIA.

Located just east of Las Vegas, Hoover Dam and the Lake Mead Recreation Area attract millions of tourists every year. Visitors to the dam itself can view the interior construction and 17-generator electric plant. Designated a National Historic Landmark in 1985.

## VIRGINIA CITY

### VIRGINIA CITY HISTORIC DISTRICT

Now a ghost town popular with tourists, originally a mining town founded in 1859 after discovery of the Comstock Lode—rich deposits of silver and gold—at nearby Mount Davidson. Virginia City flourished for about 20 years, setting an example for other Western boomtowns in the decades to come. Prospectors and speculators arrived in droves, fortunes were made overnight, and life was rowdy. Despite a fire that destroyed most of the town in 1875, it was quickly rebuilt.

Many of the historic buildings of Virginia City reflect the wealth and glory of the mining era.

Virginia City's population peaked at about 30,000 the following year. There were more than one hundred saloons at the time.

By the early 1880s, the richest mines in the area were exhausted and the price of silver had fallen drastically. Virginia City went into steady decline, eventually becoming a ghost town. Rediscovered after World War II (1939–1945) and restored

### ❖ VIRGINIA CITY ❖

- Settled in 1859 after silver and gold were discovered nearby
- A mining and agricultural village located in western Nevada, which is bordered by Oregon, Idaho, Utah, Arizona, and California
- Until 1886, Virginia City provided half of the silver mined in the United States.

to its 1870 appearance, it now features Victorian mansions on Millionaires Row, the Ponderosa Saloon, Piper's Opera House, and the Mark Twain Museum. Twain worked as a reporter for the *Territorial Enterprise*, a town newspaper in the 1860s. The historic district also includes nearby Silver City, Gold Hill, Dayton, and surrounding mining areas. Designated a National Historic Landmark in 1961.

## MORE SITES

**FORT CHURCHILL** The site of a U.S. military outpost from 1860 to 1870 that guarded mail routes, the Pony Express, and emigrant trails from attacks by Native Americans. Now a state park located in Park Silver Springs, the site includes ruins of the original adobe buildings and a visitor center. Designated a National Historic Landmark in 1961.

**FRANCIS G. NEWLANDS HOME** Located in Reno, the large Shingle-style house belonged to Francis Griffith Newlands from 1890 until his death in 1917. Newlands served as Nevada's congressman in the House of Representatives and later as a U.S. senator. He is remembered for the Reclamation Act of 1902, a law that helped spread farming to dry areas of the West through federally funded irrigation programs. The house is still privately owned. Designated a National Historic Landmark in 1963.

# NEW HAMPSHIRE

## BRETTON WOODS

**MOUNT WASHINGTON HOTEL** A luxury hotel opened in 1902 and a striking example of surviving wooden architecture. Joseph Stickney, a New Hampshire native, spared no expense when he built the grand hotel and furnished it with all the conveniences of the day—indoor plumbing, telephones, and a modern heating system. Work on the hotel continued for two years. A large porch surrounds it on almost all sides.

In 1944, more than 700 delegates—including economists, politicians, and lawyers—from 44 countries met at the Mount Washington Hotel for an international monetary conference, which became known as the Bretton Woods

The architecture of the Mount Washington Hotel includes elements of Spanish Renaissance architecture.

🌿 A town in the White Mountains of northern New Hampshire, which is bordered by Maine, Massachusetts, Vermont, the Atlantic Ocean, and the Canadian province of Quebec

🌿 Settled in the 1820s as a resort community

🌿 Site of the Mount Washington Cog Railroad, which uses toothed wheels and ratchets to climb the world's second-steepest railway passage.

Conference. The meeting established the World Bank and the International Monetary Fund, two key economic institutions that still affect the world's finances. At this meeting, the United States assumed its leading role in the world economy, which it holds today. Designated a National Historic Landmark in 1986.

## FRANKLIN

**DANIEL WEBSTER FAMILY HOME** A two-room frame house built by Ebenezer Webster around 1780 and the birthplace of Daniel Webster. Although the house

❖ F R A N K L I N ❖

🌿 Birthplace of statesman Daniel Webster on January 18, 1782

🌿 Site of a large natural mortar, which was carved by the glaciers and used by Native Americans and early settlers to grind corn; commemorated by a historical marker

itself was moved (by later owners) several times, much of it is today believed to be original. It provides an accurate look at life during colonial times.

A frail child, Daniel Webster grew up in the New Hampshire countryside. Graduating from Dartmouth College in New Hampshire in 1801, he became known as a gifted and fiery speaker. In 1807, he established a successful law practice in Portsmouth, New Hampshire. He was elected to the U.S. House of Representatives in 1812, and ten years later he was elected senator from Massachusetts. Webster went on to serve as secretary of state under Presidents Harrison, Tyler, and Fillmore—serving the country for 40 years. A forceful defender of the Union, he is perhaps best remembered for a Senate speech in January 1830: "Liberty and Union, one and inseparable, now and forever." Designated a National Historic Landmark in 1974.

## MORE SITES

**ROBERT FROST HOMESTEAD** A 13-acre (5.2-hectare) farm in Derry, New Hampshire, that was home from 1900 to 1909 to Robert Frost, a well-known poet of the twentieth century. Frost wrote 11 books of poetry and won the Pulitzer Prize four times. Today, the restored home is open to the public. Designated a National Historic Landmark in 1968.

**JOHN SULLIVAN HOUSE** Located in Durham, the home of John Sullivan, one of

George Washington's ablest military officers. Sullivan fought many battles in the New England Colonies and in the Middle Colonies. In December 1774, he captured Fort William and Mary, which guarded the entrance to Portsmouth Harbor. Sullivan bought the house in 1764 and lived there until his death in 1795. He is buried in the family cemetery near the house. Designated a National Historic Landmark in 1972.

# NEW JERSEY

## PRINCETON

**ALBERT EINSTEIN HOUSE**  The house in which the Nobel Prize–winning physicist lived from 1936 until his death in 1955. A plain white frame two-story home in the Georgian style, it includes a large front porch but has almost no yard. In later life, Einstein did most of his work at this house or at the nearby Institute for Advanced Study at Princeton. Despite his international recognition as a scientist, Einstein usually walked to the Institute from his home.

HISTORY  Einstein was born in Ulm, Germany, in 1879, but grew up in Munich. An ordinary student, Einstein attended public school and learned to play the violin. In 1900 he graduated with a general degree, planned to become a math and physics teacher, and moved to Switzerland. In 1901, he became a

❖ **P R I N C E T O N** ❖

- Founded by Quakers in 1696
- A borough located in west-central New Jersey, which is bordered by New York, Pennsylvania, Delaware, and the Atlantic Ocean
- Site of General Charles Earl Cornwallis's headquarters and the Battle of Princeton (1777)
- Meeting site of the Second Continental Congress (1775–1781)
- A leading center for education and research

Swiss citizen. While he taught, he continued his own studies, and in 1905, he received his doctoral degree from the University of Zurich in Switzerland. He published several scientific papers, one of which included his famous equation $E=mc^2$. By 1909, he was an adjunct professor of theoretical physics at Zurich University. His fame spread, and in 1914, he moved to Berlin, Germany, to continue his academic career.

In December 1932, Einstein and his wife came to the United States so that he could give a series of lectures. But in January 1933, well before the start of World War II, the dictator Adolf Hitler and the Nazis came to power in Germany. A Jew, Einstein resigned his position in Berlin, where Jews were discriminated against, and never returned to Germany. He soon joined the Institute for Advanced Study at Princeton, where he continued his scientific research.

In 1939, as World War II began, Einstein signed a letter (probably written by fellow scientists) to President Franklin D.

Roosevelt, urging the United States to develop an atomic bomb before Germany did. This letter, among other factors, helped convince Roosevelt to back the Manhattan Project, whose scientists did indeed develop the atomic bomb.

TODAY Einstein became an American citizen in 1940 and continued his work at the Institute for Advanced Study until his death in 1955. He requested that his home not become a museum. It is now owned by the Institute and is not open to the public. Designated a National Historic Landmark in 1976.

---

## TITUSVILLE

**WASHINGTON'S CROSSING** The site of George Washington's famous crossing of the Delaware River from PENNSYLVANIA into New Jersey during the American Revolution. After braving the icy waters of the river on Christmas night in 1776, Washington and his troops marched to Trenton and defeated the British forces there. The painting *Washington Crossing the Delaware* (1851), by Emanuel Gottlieb Leutze, has immortalized the event, which is depicted on the reverse side of the 2000 New Jersey state quarter.

### ❖ TITUSVILLE ❖

- Site of a 991-acre (401-hectare) New Jersey state park, situated on the Delaware River, commemorating George Washington's famous crossing in 1776

HISTORY Washington and the American troops had suffered a series of defeats in the fall of 1776 and had retreated to PENNSYLVANIA. In desperate need of both supplies and a victory, Washington planned a daring attack on Trenton, New Jersey, a town held by Hessians, German soldiers hired by the British. Knowing that the Hessians would be celebrating the Christmas holiday, Washington decided to surprise the enemy. General Washington and about 2,400 troops, in blizzard-like weather and under cover of night, crossed the ice-choked Delaware River with 18 cannons and about 200 horses.

After crossing the Delaware River, General George Washington and his staff took shelter in the Johnson Ferry House. It was here that Washington planned his attack on Trenton, a turning point of the American Revolution (1775–1783).

Washington and his troops began the dangerous nine-mile march to Trenton on icy roads. To surprise the Hessians, the troops marched in silence. Washington's men attacked in Trenton and the battle lasted about 90 minutes. Washington's army captured about 1,000 Hessian soldiers. The Hessians lost about 22 men and the colonists lost two. The stunning victory at Trenton provided Washington with much-needed supplies and raised American morale throughout the colonies.

TODAY Two state parks—one in PENNSYLVANIA and one in New Jersey—commemorate this historic event. Reenactments of the crossing and the battle are presented every year. Designated a National Historic Landmark in 1961. *See also* VIRGINIA, WASHINGTON, D.C.

---

## MORE SITES

### EDISON NATIONAL HISTORIC SITE
Located in West Orange, the site of many of Thomas Alva Edison's inventions. Edison invented or improved many items we use today—among them the telephone, sound recordings, the movie camera, and the battery. During his life, he secured 1,093 patents—rights to make or use his inventions. Edison's laboratory is today a museum open to the public. Established as a National Historic Site in 1962.

# NEW MEXICO

## ABIQUIÚ

### GEORGIA O'KEEFFE HOME AND STUDIO
An adobe compound northwest of Santa Fe where the artist Georgia O'Keeffe (1887–1986) lived and painted from 1949 to the end of her life. A native of WISCONSIN and a longtime resident of NEW YORK, O'Keeffe found artistic inspiration in the desert landscapes of northwestern New Mexico. She painted many now famous images there, such as her series of bleached cattle bones.

She settled in the old Spanish village of Abiquiú after the death of her husband, photographer Alfred Stieglitz. The house, which had been built in the 1860s, was perched above a valley and afforded spectacular views. O'Keeffe had the home restored and enlarged, creating 5,000 square feet (465 square meters) of living and work space, a large vegetable garden, and a surrounding adobe wall. The home and studio

### ❖ ABIQUIÚ ❖

- Settled in 1859 after silver and gold were discovered nearby
- Located in the foothills of the Valley Grande Mountains in northern New Mexico
- Built on the site of Pueblo ruins

were designated a National Historic Landmark in 1998 and are open to the public.

## CASA BLANCA INDIAN RESERVATION

**ACOMA PUEBLO** Native American pueblo, or village, believed to be the oldest continuously inhabited settlement in the United States. It dates to about A.D. 1100. The pueblo stands atop a sandstone mesa, or flat-topped elevation, called Adobe Rock, which made it safe from attack for centuries. Villagers descended to work in the fields below. The first Westerners to arrive were Spaniards, led by Francisco de Coronado in 1540. Spanish conquistadors destroyed much of the village in 1599, and the San Estevan de Rey Catholic mission was established there in 1629. Several Acoma families still inhabit the pueblo, which was designated a National Historic Landmark in 1960.

### ❖ CASA BLANCA ❖

🌺 Located in west-central New Mexico

🌺 About 112 miles (180 kilometers) from Santa Fe, the capital of New Mexico, which is bordered by Arizona, Utah, Colorado, Oklahoma, Texas, and the Mexican states of Sonora and Chihuahua

**TRINITY SITE** A remote desert location, at the White Sands Missile Range, where the world's first atomic bomb was exploded on July 16, 1945. The atomic bomb test device, code-named "Trinity," had been transported about 200 miles (321 kilometers) from the main research facility at Los Alamos. Designated a National Historic Landmark in 1965.

**SANTA FE PLAZA** The city's cultural, economic, and physical center, established by the Spanish during the winter of 1609–1610. The plaza first served as a defense against Native American attacks, but later it became the central market. In the 1800s, it was the final stop for pioneers traveling on the Santa Fe Trail. During the beginning of the Mexican-American War in 1846, General Stephen W. Kearney raised the American flag over the plaza, declaring it a U.S. territory. Designated a National Historic Landmark in 1960.

# NEW YORK

## NEW YORK CITY

**APOLLO THEATER** Legendary music hall and performing arts center for African Americans in the Harlem section of New York City. The Apollo played a historic role in African American music, providing a showcase for veteran and up-and-coming

- Settled in 1625 as New Amsterdam by the Dutch West India Company

- Captured by the British in 1664 and named New York after the Duke of York, the brother of King Charles II

- Located at the mouth of the Hudson River in southeastern New York, which is bordered by Vermont, Massachusetts, Connecticut, New Jersey, the Atlantic Ocean, Pennsylvania, Lakes Erie and Ontario, and the Canadian provinces of Ontario and Quebec

- Includes five boroughs: Manhattan, the Bronx, Queens, Brooklyn, and Staten Island

- The largest port and city in the United States, New York served as the first United States capital (1785–1790) and state capital (1784–1797).

**BROOKLYN BRIDGE** Suspension bridge connecting the boroughs of Brooklyn and Manhattan over the East River in New York City. Its span of 1,595 feet (486 meters) made it the world's longest suspension bridge for 20 years. Dedicated on May 24, 1883, the Brooklyn Bridge was one of the great engineering and artistic achievements of the late nineteenth century.

The mainstays of the bridge are two granite towers, each 271 feet (83 meters) high. The span is suspended by thick steel cables that extend from each end and hang between the towers. Hundreds of stay cables radiate from each tower, creating the appearance of a giant web. The cables are made of hundreds of steel wires

Spanning the East River, the Brooklyn Bridge connects the Island of Manhattan with Brooklyn. The roadbed is 135 feet (41.14 meters) above the river.

singers, jazz musicians, and comedians. During its heyday from the 1930s through the 1950s, it featured such established and future stars as Count Basie, Billie Holiday, Sarah Vaughan, Dinah Washington, Aretha Franklin, and Ella Fitzgerald. Many music legends got their first big break in the Apollo's weekly "Amateur Nights." Located on 125th Street between 7th and 8th Avenues, it was the heart of the Harlem Renaissance cultural movement during the first half of the twentieth century.

After falling into decline during the 1960s, the theater closed its doors in the 1970s. It underwent a major renovation and was reopened in 1983. Listed in the National Register of Historic Places in 1983.

The Chrysler Building took fewer than two years to complete. The 77-story building includes 200 flights of stairs.

between Brooklyn and lower Manhattan. In 1983, on the occasion of its hundredth anniversary, the beloved bridge was honored with a fireworks display and harbor parade. Designated a National Historic Landmark in 1964. *See also* WEST VIRGINIA.

**CHRYSLER BUILDING** Skyscraper of architectural distinction at Lexington Avenue and 42nd Street in Manhattan. It is considered an outstanding example of Art Deco design, a sleek decorative style popular from about 1920 to 1940. Designed by William Van Alen and built by the automobile manufacturer Walter Chrysler, the structure was completed in 1930.

spun together. It was the longest suspension bridge for its time.

The structure was designed between 1867 and 1869 by John A. Roebling, who died in an accident a year before construction began. His son, Washington Roebling, supervised the project from 1870 to completion 13 years later. The bridge, which cost $9 million to build, carried cable cars, trolley cars, the elevated railroad, and pedestrians.

Today, its six lanes of traffic continue to provide a vital link

★ PROFILE ★
## BILLIE HOLIDAY

**B**orn Eleanor Fagan in Baltimore, MARYLAND, Billie Holiday (1915–1959) is regarded as the finest and most original jazz singer of her era. Raised in poverty, she moved to New York City as a teenager to live with her mother. She began singing at small nightclubs and eventually at the Apollo Theater in Harlem; performed with several well-known big bands, including the Count Basie Orchestra; and recorded songs with the great Benny Goodman and Duke Ellington. By the end of the 1930s, she was a major star. Her vocal style, known as "swing-song" has influenced generations of jazz singers. Holiday recounted her often unhappy life in the 1956 autobiography *Lady Sings the Blues*.

Resting on a wide base several stories high, the structure rises in steps to ever narrower heights. The building is topped by a stainless steel pyramid-shaped crown, with arches of diminishing size and a needlepoint tower. The main lobby, of elaborate marble-and-chrome design, is itself an exquisite example of Art Deco style. Designated a National Historic Landmark in 1976.

**TENEMENT BUILDING AT 97 ORCHARD STREET** Brick apartment building on Manhattan's Lower East Side that was home to thousands of newly arrived immigrants between 1863 and 1935. The six-story row house was typical of the cramped tenements built for New York's first great wave of immigrants. During its 72 years of existence, the building housed some 7,000 people from more than 20 countries. It fell into disrepair during the Great Depression, and the tenants were evicted in 1935.

The tenement remained boarded up until 1988, when a major renovation was begun. Today, the building houses the Lower East Side Tenement Museum, which is dedicated to the millions of struggling immigrants who arrived in New York. (In 1900, some two-thirds of the city's population—most of them immigrants—lived on the Lower East Side.) Visitors can tour authentically restored apartments and learn about the actual residents. Designated a National Historic Landmark in 1994.

**VASSAR COLLEGE OBSERVATORY** The college's original astronomical observatory, built in 1865 for Professor Maria Mitchell. The facility was custom designed for Mitchell's use. A solid brick building in the middle of campus, the observatory was topped by a large dome with rollback shutters for telescopic viewing. It housed the world's third largest telescope at the time. The building also contained a

A bust of Maria Mitchell, who viewed the stars from the Vassar observatory, pays tribute to America's first woman astronomer.

- Settled in 1867 by the Dutch
- Located on the Hudson River in southeastern New York
- Served as state capital in 1777
- Site of New York's ratification of the United States Constitution in 1788

classroom, laboratory, and Mitchell's personal residence.

The original observatory eventually grew obsolete, no longer meeting the needs of modern astronomers. In 1997, it was replaced by a new facility at the edge of the campus. The new observatory houses three reflecting telescopes in three separate domes. The old observatory is still standing, but is no longer used, and it is not open to the public. Designated a National Historic Landmark in 1991.

## ROCHESTER

**SUSAN B. ANTHONY HOUSE** Home of the women's rights pioneer for the last 40 years of her life, beginning in 1866. The red-brick, ivy-covered house, which

- Settled in 1812 by Colonel Nathaniel Rochester
- Site of a stop on the Underground Railroad
- An industrial city that is a major center in the production of photographic, photocopying, optical, and dental equipment

she shared with her sister Mary, was Anthony's residence during her most politically active years. When she was not away campaigning for women's suffrage, she wrote, organized, and met with other activists at her house on Madison Street.

Now a museum, the house contains many of Anthony's original furnishings and personal memorabilia. A special collection on the second floor recounts the history of the women's suffrage movement. Designated a National Historic Landmark in 1965.

## MORE SITES

**ERIE CANAL** Historic inland waterway that established an economically vital barge connection between Albany on the Hudson River and Buffalo on Lake Erie. The original 353-mile (585-kilometer) canal, built between 1817 and 1825, was a major engineering feat for its time. By connecting the Atlantic Seaboard with the Great Lakes, it was also a key factor in the settlement of the Northwest Territory. Designated a National Historic Landmark in 1960.

**NIAGARA RESERVATION** A state park created in 1885. Covering 435 acres (176 hectares) on the Niagara River, the reservation was set aside for its natural beauty—especially for its views of Niagara Falls—and to protect its plant and animal life. Designated a National Historic Landmark in 1963.

# NORTH CAROLINA

## ASHEVILLE

**BILTMORE ESTATE** Located in Asheville, the 250-room mansion of George Washington Vanderbilt. While traveling through the mountains of western North Carolina, Vanderbilt was awed by the natural beauty of the area. He decided to build his estate there and bought 125,000 acres (50,585 hectares) of land.

HISTORY Created to look like a French chateau, the house was designed by the well-known architect, Richard Morris Hunt. Construction began in 1889. Vanderbilt moved into the mansion in 1895, but work continued for several more years. The house included 34 master bedrooms, 43 bathrooms, 3 kitchens, and 65 fireplaces. In addition, the house boasted all the modern conveniences of the day—hot water, indoor plumbing, central heating, electricity, and mechanical refrigeration.

The vast gardens of the estate were designed by Frederick Law Olmsted, the famous landscape architect who also designed Central Park in New York City. Olmsted recommended that the woodlands around Biltmore, including the Pisgah Woods, be kept natural and not developed into a formal park. Later, these woods were sold to the federal government and became the basis for the Pisgah National Forest. Over time, other properties were also sold. Today, the estate owns about 8,000 acres (3,237 hectares).

## ❖ ASHEVILLE ❖

- A city located in western North Carolina, which is bordered by Virginia, Tennessee, Georgia, South Carolina, and the Atlantic Ocean

- About 250 miles (402 kilometers) from Raleigh, the state capital

- Four United States Navy ships have been named for the city of Asheville

The acres of gardens at Biltmore Estate include a vast variety of spring flowers such as tulips, dogwoods, redbuds, forsythia, magnolia, and flowering cherries.

TODAY Biltmore opened to the public in 1930 to help draw Depression-era tourists to the region, but it remains family owned. The estate and gardens remain open to the public. Each year, about 900,000 visitors come to admire the priceless antiques, rare art, and 250 acres (101 hectares) of gardens and formal grounds. Designated a National Historic Landmark in 1963.

## HATTERAS

### CAPE HATTERAS LIGHT STATION

A lighthouse on Cape Hatteras on the Outer Banks of North Carolina. Because the sandy beaches of the Outer Banks are dangerous to ships, the first lighthouse was built in the area in 1803. Its height was raised several times, until the current lighthouse was built in 1870. At 208 feet (63.4 meters), it is the tallest lighthouse in the nation.

The lighthouse has been threatened by erosion since it was built. In 1870, the water was about 1,300 feet (396 meters) away. By 1935, it had moved to just 100 feet (30.5 meters) away. Because of the danger, a temporary lighthouse was built in 1936. By 1950, erosion was no longer deemed a threat, and the Cape Hatteras Light Station returned to service.

Erosion again threatened in the 1990s. The lighthouse was moved about 2,900 feet (884 meters) inland in 1999—being pushed inch by inch. The move took 23 days. The lighthouse is a popular tourist attraction, but at night it still helps guide sailors around the dangerous Outer Banks. Designated a National Historic Landmark in 1998.

### ❖ HATTERAS ❖

- A village about 13 miles (4 kilometers) south of Cape Hatteras, on the east coast of North Carolina
- The Lost Colony of Roanoke, settled in 1585, was located just to the north of Hatteras.

## MORE SITES

### WRIGHT BROTHERS NATIONAL MEMORIAL

The site of the Wright Brothers' first successful flight on December 17, 1903, in Kitty Hawk, North Carolina. At the top of 90-foot (27-meter) Kill Devil Hill is a 60-foot (18-meter) tall granite memorial noting the OHIO brothers' success. The aircraft, the 1903 *Wright Flyer*, hangs in the Smithsonian Air and Space Museum in WASHINGTON, D.C. Established as a National Memorial in 1953.

### OLD SALEM HISTORIC DISTRICT

Located in Winston–Salem, a community settled by Moravians from PENNSYLVANIA in 1766. The architecture of the buildings reflects the German heritage of the original settlers. Designated a National Historic Landmark in 1966.

# NORTH DAKOTA

## STANTON

**KNIFE RIVER INDIAN VILLAGES NATIONAL HISTORIC SITE** Native American settlement near present-day Stanton in west-central North Dakota. It dates back at least 8,000 years. Nomadic hunters used flint from the Knife River to make weapons, and later tribes used the material for trade. The Lewis and Clark expedition visited three Hidatsa villages there in October 1804 and spent the winter at nearby Fort Mandan. It was there that the young Shoshone woman Sacagawea joined them as a guide. The settlement was last occupied by Hidatsa and Mandan Native Americans in 1845. Today, it features a visitor center, research facility, and the remains of earth lodges at three village sites. Established as a National Historic Site in 1974.

**FORT UNION TRADING POST NATIONAL HISTORIC SITE** The most important fur-trading depot on the upper Missouri River for nearly four decades. It was built in Williston in 1828 by the American Fur Trading Company and taken down in 1867. Native Americans throughout the region brought beaver and buffalo hides in exchange for goods. The arrival of steamboats up the Missouri in the 1830s helped make Fort Union the center of a vast trading network. The introduction of whiskey and smallpox by white traders strained relations with the local people. The United States Army purchased the depot in the 1860s and used the timber to build nearby Fort Buford. Established as a National Historic Site in 1966.

The Knife River Indian Villages National Historic Site in the photo above helps us understand the native peoples of the American plains.

### ❖ STANTON ❖

🌿 Located in west-central North Dakota

🌿 About 65 miles (104.6 kilometers) from Bismarck, the capital of North Dakota, which is bordered by Minnesota, South Dakota, Montana, and the Canadian provinces of Manitoba and Saskatchewan

### ❖ WILLISTON ❖

🌿 Incorporated in 1904

🌿 A city on the Missouri River in northwestern North Dakota

🌿 Initially a riverboating town, Williston grew with the arrival of the Great Northern Railroad (1887) and the discovery of rich oil reserves (1951).

### ADAMS-FAIRVIEW BONANZA FARM

A Wahpeton wheat farm and summer-house founded in 1881. Like other "bonanza" farms in the Red River Valley, it was established on cheap land sold by the railroad to showcase the economic promise of the area. Today, it is a privately run bed-and-breakfast. Listed in the National Register of Historic Places in 1990.

### UKRAINIAN IMMIGRANT DWELLINGS AND CHURCHES

Settlements dating from about 1900 to 1940 in the western part of the state. Ukrainians were among the last immigrants to settle in North Dakota, where their cultural heritage remains strong. Listed in the National Register of Historic Places in 1987.

# OHIO

## CLEVELAND

**CLEVELAND ARCADE** One of the few remaining glass-covered shopping centers in the nation. Glass-covered shopping arcades were the forerunners to today's indoor shopping malls.

Construction of the Cleveland Arcade, located in the center of downtown Cleveland, began in 1888 and was completed in 1890. Five levels of shops and galleries surround the 300-foot (91.4-meter) long esplanade, or center mall. A highly detailed glass-and-steel skylight—soaring 104 feet (31.6 meters) above the floor—encloses the arcade. An architectural wonder when completed, the Cleveland Arcade has changed little over time and remains a vibrant shopping area in the heart of downtown. Designated a National Historic Landmark in 1975.

### ❖ CLEVELAND ❖

- Cleveland received its village charter in 1814, although European settlers lived in the area as early as the 1790s.
- Became a city in 1836 and started its first public schools
- Located in northeastern Ohio, which is bordered by Pennsylvania, West Virginia, Kentucky, Indiana, Michigan, and Lake Erie
- President-elect Abraham Lincoln visited Cleveland in February 1861 on his way to his inauguration.

Ironwork encircles the entire fifth level of the Cleveland Arcade, whose construction was partly financed by the oil millionaire John D. Rockefeller and by the wealthy politician Mark Hanna.

**WRIGHT FLYER III** A wood-and-muslin fabric aircraft, designed and flown by Wilber and Orville Wright, and the first true airplane. After the initial success of the first flight on December 17, 1903, at Kitty Hawk, NORTH CAROLINA, the Wright brothers continued to improve the designs of their aircraft. The Wright Brothers' first planes were difficult to control and frequently crashed.

The *Wright Flyer III* made its first flight at Huffman Prairie in Dayton, Ohio, in 1905. This plane could be steered, make turns, and be controlled in a gust of wind. Soon, the plane was modified to hold a passenger. Later versions of the *Wright Flyer III* reached speeds of 45 miles per hour (72 kilometers per hour), soared to an altitude of 360 feet (107.9 meters), and covered a distance of 77 miles (124 kilometers).

Because the Wright Brothers did not

### ❖ DAYTON ❖

- ❧ General William Rogers Clark brought about 1,000 settlers to the site of present-day Dayton in 1780.
- ❧ In 1810, Dayton had a permanent population of 383.
- ❧ Regular stagecoach service between Cincinnati and Dayton began in 1816—the trip took two days.
- ❧ In 1913, a horrible flood claimed between 300 and 400 lives and caused $100 million in damage in a few hours.

consider the *Wright Flyer III* worthy of preservation, it was dismantled and its parts were displayed in many locations. Finally, in 1947, with direction from Orville Wright, the plane was reassembled, although some new parts had to be created. The original *Wright Flyer*, which flew at Kitty Hawk, NORTH CAROLINA, hangs in the Smithsonian Air and Space Museum in WASHINGTON, D.C. The *Wright Flyer III* is on display in Wright Hall at Dayton's Carillon Park. Designated a National Historic Landmark in 1990.

### MORE SITES

**JAMES A. GARFIELD NATIONAL HISTORIC SITE** Known as Lawnfield, the Mentor, Ohio, home of the twentieth president of the United States. Garfield purchased the home in 1876 and lived there until he moved to WASHINGTON, D.C., in 1881. Garfield campaigned for the presidency from his front porch. Today, the home is open to the public as a museum. Established as a National Historic Site in 1980.

**OHIO STATEHOUSE** Located in the capital of Columbus, one of the best examples of Greek Revival architecture in the United States. Begun in 1839, Ohio's limestone capitol was not completed until 1861. The center of the building, a cylindrical shape, is unusual because it is not capped by a dome. Designated a National Historic Landmark in 1977.

# OKLAHOMA

## LAWTON

**FORT SILL** United States Army post established in 1869 as a cavalry base for operations against Native Americans. Built under the direction of General Philip H. Sheridan, a Union hero in the Civil War (1861–1865), Fort Sill played an important role in campaigns against the Southern Plains peoples for more than two decades. The fort was named for Brigadier General Joshua W. Sill, a friend of Sheridan who was killed in the Civil War. Original buildings were constructed by black troops of the 10th Cavalry, known as the Buffalo Soldiers. Now vastly expanded, Fort Sill remains important as the home of the Army Field Artillery Center and Field Artillery School. Designated a National Historic Landmark in 1960.

### ★ PROFILE ★
### SEQUOYAH

A Cherokee scholar and silversmith, Sequoyah (also known as George Guess, 1766–1843) invented a written version of the Cherokee language. The system, called "talking leaves," uses 86 characters to represent every sound in the Cherokee tongue. Sequoyah's work enabled thousands of tribe members to learn to read and write. He traveled to western Cherokee settlements to teach his new system. Beginning in 1828, it was used to publish a weekly newspaper called the *Cherokee Phoenix*.

### ❖ LAWTON ❖

- Incorporated in 1901
- Located in southwestern Oklahoma, which is bordered by Colorado, Kansas, Missouri, Arkansas, Texas, and New Mexico
- A commercial and trading center of cotton, wheat, and cattle for the surrounding area and Fort Sill

### TAHLEQUAH

**CHEROKEE NATIONAL CAPITOL** Meeting place for the government of the Cherokee Nation from 1869 to 1907. The Cherokee had adopted a constitution and

A fountain stands in front of the historic Cherokee National Capitol. Today, the Cherokee Nation is run from a sprawling complex of buildings just south of Tahlequah.

- Settled by the Cherokee in 1839
- Located in eastern Oklahoma
- A commercial and trade center for growing fruit and agricultural products as well as raising livestock

unified democratic government in the 1820s. Tahlequah became the Cherokee capital in the 1830s and remains so today. The two-story Victorian brick building, located in downtown Tahlequah, was the center of Cherokee efforts to maintain peaceful relations with whites and to retain tribal lands. In the last decades of the nineteenth century, however, the government took away more Cherokee land and rights. When Oklahoma was granted statehood in 1907, the capitol became the Cherokee County Court House. Designated a National Historic Landmark in 1961.

## MORE SITES

**NELLIE JOHNSTONE NO. 1** The first commercial oil well in what is now the state of Oklahoma, drilled in 1897. (It was then Indian Territory.) A geyser of gushing crude oil on April 15, 1897, marked the beginning of Oklahoma's oil boom. The well got its name from the young daughter of one of its financiers. A replica marks the original site near Bartlesville. Listed in the National Register of Historic Places in 1972.

**GUTHRIE HISTORIC DISTRICT** A group of commercial buildings built between 1889 and 1910 in Guthrie. The red-brick and sandstone buildings reflect the city founders' vision for Guthrie, which was the territorial capital of Oklahoma from 1890 to 1907 and the first state capital from 1907 to 1910. Designated a National Historic Landmark in 1999.

# OREGON

## JACKSONVILLE

**JACKSONVILLE HISTORIC DISTRICT** A mining town that boomed after the discovery of gold in 1852. It was the seat of Jackson County and the center of business and finance in southern Oregon for 32 years.

Thousands of miners flocked to the foothills of the Klamath (or Siskiyou) Mountains after the discovery of gold at Rich Gulch. The mining camp in Rogue

❖ JACKSONVILLE ❖

- A gold rush town founded in 1852
- Located in southwestern Oregon, which is bordered by Washington, Idaho, Nevada, California, and the Pacific Ocean
- A fine example of a mid-nineteenth century inland commercial and mining community in the Pacific Northwest

Valley quickly grew into the bustling town of Jacksonville. Stores, banks, saloons, and gambling halls sprang up as more prospectors and investors arrived. Wealthy merchants built grand houses. However, many residents and businesses moved away after the California and Medford Railroad bypassed the town in 1884. By the 1890s, agriculture had replaced mining as the area's main industry. In 1927, Medford replaced Jacksonville as the county seat, further contributing to the town's decline.

Residents of Jacksonville, recognizing the historic interest and architectural beauty of the town, worked for decades to preserve its buildings and public spaces. More than 80 residential, commercial, and civic structures have been restored to their original conditions. Notable among these are the C.C. Beekman Bank, U.S. Hotel, and Wells Fargo office. Photos, artifacts, and writings from boomtown days are on display in the Jacksonville Museum, formerly the county courthouse. The Jacksonville district is a time capsule of a thriving Western community in the mid-1800s. Designated a National Historic Landmark in 1966.

## MOUNT HOOD NATIONAL FOREST

**TIMBERLINE LODGE** A rustic resort hotel on the southern slope of Mount Hood, at an elevation of 6,000 feet (1,830 meters) above sea level. The Works Progress Administration (WPA), a work-relief program of the New Deal, hired unemployed craftspeople who built the Timberline Lodge between 1936 and 1937. (The WPA provided useful jobs for unemployed workers during the Great Depression.) Made of giant timbers and native stone and decorated with fanciful carvings, the building is considered a masterpiece of "mountain architecture." It is designed to withstand heavy wind and deep snow while blending in with the natural landscape. The lodge is located in Mount Hood National Forest, about halfway to the mountain summit, affording dramatic views of the Cascade Mountain range to the south. Its name is synonymous with the tree line, the altitude at which trees can no longer grow.

The rustic Timberline Lodge took only 15 months to complete. It was built entirely by hand.

The Timberline Lodge remains a popular year-round resort, with 70 rooms, skiing and snowboarding areas, hiking and climbing terrain, and other facilities for outdoor recreation and indoor relaxation. Designated a National Historic Landmark in 1977.

## ❖ MOUNT HOOD ❖

- Named for the nearby volcano
- Located about 121 miles (194.7 kilometers) from Salem, the capital of Oregon
- Tourism is the major industry.

## MORE SITES

**FORT ASTORIA SITE** Trading station at the mouth of the Columbia River, founded by John Jacob Astor's Pacific Fur Company in 1811. Though sold to the British two years later, it was the first American settlement west of the Rocky Mountains. A reconstructed timber blockhouse now stands at the downtown Astoria site. Designated a National Historic Landmark in 1961.

**SKIDMORE OLD TOWN HISTORIC DISTRICT** A 20-block site where the city of Portland began. Most buildings in the area date from the Victorian era of the mid-to-late nineteenth century. The Skidmore Fountain, erected in 1888 in the center of town, gives the district its name. Designated a National Historic Landmark in 1977.

# PENNSYLVANIA

## GETTYSBURG

**GETTYSBURG NATIONAL MILITARY PARK** Located about 140 miles (225 kilometers) west of Philadelphia, the site of the turning point of the Civil War (1861–1865), where a fierce battle raged from July 1 to July 3, 1863. The Battle of Gettysburg was the bloodiest battle of the Civil War, with about 51,000 troops, killed, wounded, or captured.

**HISTORY** Seeking a decisive victory, General Robert E. Lee, the commander of the Confederate Army, decided to invade the North for a second time. Lee and his troops were also desperate for supplies. As Lee moved toward the North, a Union army under the command of General George G. Meade shadowed Lee's army. An accidental encounter between the two sides quickly burst into a bloody battle.

### ❖ GETTYSBURG ❖

- Located in southeastern Pennsylvania, which is bordered by New Jersey, Delaware, Maryland, West Virginia, Ohio, New York, and Lake Erie
- William Penn's family purchased the city's land from the Iroquois in 1736.
- The city is named for James Gettys and his son Samuel Gettys, early settlers from the 1760s.
- In 1860, three years before the famous battle, the town had about 2,400 residents.

General Meade's army quickly established strong positions on the hills to the south and west of Gettysburg. Lee, though his troops were outnumbered, was confident of victory. Bloody fighting raged as each side attempted to win. On July 3, in what is known as Pickett's Charge, Confederate troops made a last attempt at victory. Thousands of soldiers were killed in an attack that lasted less than one hour. Lee lost about one-third of his army. The Battle of Gettysburg was the South's last attempt to invade the North, and Lee's army retreated back to VIRGINIA.

The Gettysburg National Military Park includes Gettysburg National Cemetery, where about 3,500 Civil War soldiers are buried. In November 1863, President Abraham Lincoln visited the cemetery and solemnly dedicated it. His words—the Gettysburg Address—inspired the nation.

TODAY Today, the battlefield commemorates the thousands who died there. The park includes 6,000 acres (2,428 hectares), 26 miles (41.8 kilometers) of roads, and more than 1,400 monuments and statues, many by leading American sculptors. It is now the final resting place for soldiers from all major wars. The site is closed to new burials. The park became a National Military Park in 1895.

More than 1,300 monuments dot the Gettysburg battlefield. The Pennsylvania Monument features bronze tablets listing the regiments and names of the more than 34,000 Pennsylvanians who fought in the Gettysburg campaign.

## HERSHEY

**MILTON S. HERSHEY MANSION** From 1908 to 1945, the home of Milton S. Hershey, who revolutionized and popularized the chocolate bar. The Colonial Revival home on Chocolate Avenue was made from local limestone. Hershey donated the house to a country club in 1930, and he continued to live in a small second-floor apartment. In 1977, the Hershey Chocolate Company bought the building, and today it is the corporate headquarters of the company—one of the world's largest makers of chocolate and other candy.

## ❖ HERSHEY ❖

- In 1905, Milton S. Hershey opened the first modern chocolate factory in Pennsylvania's farmlands.

- The Hotel Hershey, a world-class resort, opened in 1933.

- The Hershey Zoo, opened in 1916, is now ZooAmerica, an 11-acre (4.45-hectare) zoo that specializes in the animals of North America.

HISTORY Although best known for chocolate, Hershey, once apprenticed to a candy maker, began his own career making caramels. A few years after starting his caramel business, he opened the Hershey Chocolate Company to make a coating for the caramels.

He sold the caramel business for $1 million and devoted his life to chocolate. In 1900, he began making the Hershey Bar. Hershey established a town for his employees that included affordable homes, a public transportation system, and schools, including a school for orphaned boys. To help create a pleasant work environment, Hershey established a park for his employees. Originally a simple green space in which to picnic and play ball, it has grown into a vast amusement park with dozens of rides and attractions and a zoo.

TODAY The company and the town founded by Milton Hershey is famous throughout the world. The town, the chocolate factory, and the amusement park are open to visitors throughout the year. Other special events, including hot-air ballooning and an antique car show, also bring tourists to Hershey. Designated a National Historic Landmark in 1983.

## PHILADELPHIA

**FIRST BANK OF THE UNITED STATES** Located in Philadelphia, the site of the country's first national bank. Designed in the neoclassical style by amateur architect Samuel Blodgett and built between

★ PROFILE ★

### WILLIAM PENN

Although born in England, William Penn had a great influence on American history. Penn was a Quaker, or "Friend," a religious group that believes in the equality of men and women and opposes violence of any kind. In 1681, Penn convinced King Charles II to grant him a huge tract of land in England's American colonies as payment for a debt. Penn wanted to settle the new colony as a haven for Quakers and other religious groups. He named the colony Pennsylvania, which means "Penn's woods."

After Penn and his fellow colonists arrived in America, he bought land from the Native Americans and strived to live in peace. He also planned and named the city of Philadelphia, which means "City of Brotherly Love." Penn spent much of his life working to make his colony a success. By the 1700s, Pennsylvania was one of the largest of the 13 colonies, and Philadelphia was one the colonies' leading cities.

1794 and 1797, it is likely the first use of marble on the façade of a major building in the United States.

The establishment of the First Bank of the United States caused the first major controversy of George Washington's presidency (1788–1797). The United States Constitution does not specifically allow for the creation of a bank. Led by Secretary of the Treasury Alexander Hamilton, "loose constructionists" claimed that the authority to create a bank was implied in the power to print and coin money. Secretary of State Thomas Jefferson led opposition to the bank. These "strict constructionists" claimed that the national government had no powers except those specifically listed in the Constitution. Washington eventually sided with Hamilton, and the bank went forward. Congress allowed the bank's charter to expire in 1811. The bank building was restored for the nation's Bicentennial in 1976, but it is usually closed to

❖ PHILADELPHIA ❖

- William Penn, a Quaker, bought the land on which Philadelphia is located from the Leni Lenape (Delaware) chiefs in 1682.
- The city is nicknamed "The City of Brotherly Love."
- Penn planned his city and published the first map in 1683.
- The largest city in Pennsylvania
- Philadelphia served as the second capital of the United States from 1790 to 1800.

the public. Designated a National Historic Landmark in 1987.

VALLEY FORGE

**VALLEY FORGE NATIONAL HISTORIC PARK** Located about 18 miles (28.9 kilometers) northwest of Philadelphia, the site where General George Washington and American troops spent the bitter winter of 1777–1778. The troops—cold, tired, hungry, and ill-trained—entered the camp on December 19, 1777.

Conditions at Valley Forge were desperate as soldiers quickly built huts for shelter from the snow and wind. Clothing and blankets were scarce, and the troops' frostbitten bare feet left trails of blood in the snow. Food was in short supply, and the men often survived on "firecake," a tasteless mix of flour and water. Hundreds of horses starved to death. Washington wrote to the Continental Congress, America's governing body at the time, for supplies, but little help was available. About 2,000 soldiers died.

After enduring these extreme hardships, the Americans emerged in June 1778 a skilled fighting force, thanks to training and drilling by Baron von Steuben. Von Steuben, once an elite officer in the Prussian army, offered his services to the Patriot cause. Washington recognized his military skills and asked him to train the forces.

Today, that winter at Valley Forge is remembered as a symbol of America's dedication and commitment to the cause

A solitary cannon symbolizes the suffering of Washington's troops at Valley Forge.

**INDEPENDENCE HALL AND NATIONAL HISTORIC PARK** Located in downtown Philadelphia, a Georgian-style building commissioned in 1732 and the site of the signing of the Declaration of Independence (1776) and the United States Constitution (1787). Today, Independence Hall is part of the National Park Service and is open to the public daily. Became a National Park in 1966.

**LIBERTY BELL** The Liberty Bell is located in Independence National Park. Originally cast in 1751, the bell was hung in the steeple of the Philadelphia State House (now Independence Hall). It was rung on July 8, 1776, to announce the first reading of the Declaration of Independence. The bell cracked while tolling to commemorate George Washington's birthday in 1846.

of liberty. The Valley Forge Park grounds are open to visitors year round. Became a National Historic Park in 1976.

### ❖ VALLEY FORGE ❖

- Named for a nearby iron forge on Valley Creek
- No battles were fought at Valley Forge, but about 2,000 soldiers died from starvation and disease during the harsh winter of 1777–1778.

**JOHNSTOWN INCLINED RAILWAY** A cable-driven railway constructed after the 1889 Johnstown Flood to serve as a safe way to carry people and vehicles out of the valley to higher ground. The convenience of the railway is responsible for the growth of Westmont, one of the country's first suburbs. Today, the operating railway is part of a visitor center owned by the Cambria County Transit Authority. Listed in the National Register of Historic Places in 1973.

# RHODE ISLAND

## NEWPORT

**OLD STATE HOUSE** Also called the Old Colony House, a historically and architecturally significant building dating to 1739. A two-and-a-half-story brick structure, it is considered one of the finest examples of early Georgian architecture in the United States. It was designed by Richard Munday and built under the direction of Benjamin Wyatt. The second-oldest state capitol in the country, it was built to house the Rhode Island General Assembly. From 1790 to 1900, it served as one of the state's two capitols. (The Rhode Island legislature alternated sessions in another building in Providence.)

The Old State House was the site of many notable events in the history of colonial Newport. On July 20, 1776, residents gathered under the balcony to hear a reading of the new Declaration of Independence. In 1782, General George Washington attended a banquet given in his honor by France's Comte de Rochambeau in the Great Hall. And in May 1790, colonial delegates met in the building to ratify the United States Constitution.

The Old State House served as a county court from 1900 to 1926. Today, the stately building on Washington Square is open for public viewing. Designated a National Historic Landmark in 1960.

## ❖ NEWPORT ❖

🍂 Founded in 1639

🍂 A leading mercantile seaport in the eighteenth century

🍂 A nineteenth-century resort town located in southeast Rhode Island, which is bordered by Massachusetts, Connecticut, Block Island Sound, and Rhode Island Sound

🍂 For more than a century, Rhode Island had two capitals: Providence and Newport. Providence became the sole state capital in 1900.

🍂 With the British occupation of Newport during the American Revolution, many buildings were destroyed, and most citizens moved away. The city never regained its trading prestige, but from the 1830s onward, it became a summer resort.

## PAWTUCKET

**OLD SLATER MILL** The first successful cotton mill in the United States and the birthplace of the nation's textile industry. Samuel Slater, an immigrant who had worked in an English textile plant, established the Pawtucket factory in 1793. He set up the mill with two partners (William Almy and Moses Brown) and reconstructed the complicated machinery from memory. The water-powered facility is located on the Blackstone River. The main source of power was a large waterwheel that turned overhead shafts inside the mill. The shafts, in turn, powered machines used to card (clean, disentangle, and collect) the raw cotton and then spin

Old Slater Mill, now restored to its 1830 appearance, stands next to the Blackstone River, which once powered the mill's machines.

- Located at Pawtucket Falls in north-eastern Rhode Island
- Deeded to Roger Williams in 1638, Pawtucket was a haven for religious freedom in New England.
- Known as the "cradle of the American textile industry"

process. The Old Slater Mill was enlarged several times over the years and restored in 1924. It is now a museum of textiles and early manufacturing. Designated a National Historic Landmark in 1966.

it into yarn to make cloth. (The spinning machines were called mules.) Slater went on to build textile mills at other sites in New England.

Pawtucket, then a village within the town of New Providence, is often called the birthplace of the Industrial Revolution in America. Slater's mill was the first facility to rely on power-driven machines. It also pioneered the factory system of manufacturing, in which large groups of workers were brought together under one roof and carried out specific tasks in a coordinated

## MORE SITES

**BELLEVUE AVENUE HISTORIC DISTRICT, NEWPORT** Location of palatial summer homes—misleadingly called "cottages"—built by wealthy industrialists in the late nineteenth and early twentieth centuries. The diverse styles represent the work of some of America's most notable architects. Designated a National Historic Landmark in 1976.

**FLYING HORSE CAROUSEL** One of the oldest carousels of its kind in the United States, dating from 1876 to 1879 in Watch Hill. Twenty horses, each carved from a single wood block, have tails and mains made of real horsehair. They are not attached to the platform but are suspended from a center frame by an arm that swings out during the ride. Designated a National Historic Landmark in 1987.

# SOUTH CAROLINA

## CHARLESTON

A single cannon helps commemorate the Union troops' defense of Fort Sumter. The battle lasted 34 hours, but no one was killed.

**FORT SUMTER** United States military fortification in Charleston harbor where the first shots in the Civil War were fired on April 12, 1861. Construction of the fort began in 1829 and continued until South Carolina seceded from the Union in 1860. After the state had seceded, the federal government retained possession of Fort Sumter and two other garrisons in the harbor. South Carolina state troops captured the two other strongholds, as Major Robert Anderson concentrated federal forces at Fort Sumter. The North and South were unsuccessful in negotiating a peaceful evacuation, and Confederate leaders finally ordered General P.G.T. Beauregard to launch an attack. The first shot was fired at 4:30 A.M. on April 12, 1861. Anderson was forced to surrender on April 14, and the United States declared war on the Confederacy the following day. Fort Sumter remained in Confederate hands until February 1865.

Located on Sullivan Island, Fort Sumter is a five-sided brick structure. It is named for Thomas Sumter, a military leader in the American Revolution (1775–1783). Administered by the National Park Service; became a national monument in 1948.

**KAHAL KADOSH BETH ELOHIM** Synagogue recognized as the birthplace of Reform Judaism in America. Its Hebrew

### ❖ CHARLESTON ❖

- Founded by the British in 1680, Charleston is the oldest city in South Carolina, which is bordered by North Carolina, Georgia, and the Atlantic Ocean.
- Located in southeast South Carolina on a peninsula in Charleston harbor
- In colonial times, it was the capital of South Carolina.
- Captured by the British (1780–1782) and blockaded by Union troops (1860–1865)

name means "Holy Congregation House of God." Reform Judaism is a progressive movement in the Jewish faith that modernized traditional worship by allowing recitation of translated prayers, music in religious services, women rabbis, and other innovations.

The original building—then the largest synagogue in the United States—was completed in 1799 and destroyed in the great Charleston fire of 1838. In the meantime, liberal members of the congregation had organized the Reformed Society of Israelites in 1824. The new Beth Elohim synagogue, a monumental Greek Revival structure, was built between 1840 and 1841. An organ was installed, and Beth Elohim became the first Reform congregation in the United States. It is the third-oldest functioning synagogue in the country. Designated a National Historic Landmark in 1980.

## STONO RIVER SLAVE REBELLION SITE

Riverbank location southwest of Charleston where 20 escaped slaves launched an armed revolt on September 9, 1739. Led by a native Angolan named Jemmy, they attacked a nearby store, killed the two proprietors, and seized the guns inside. Gathering recruits as they traveled south, they burned plantation houses and killed whites. Chanting "Liberty!" and marching to the rhythm of African drums, a band of nearly one hundred set out for freedom in Spanish Florida. Local militia caught up with the slaves late that same afternoon, killing or capturing all of them.

The Stono River rebellion was the largest slave uprising in America prior to independence. As a result, colonial lawmakers passed strict new rules on the behavior of enslaved people. Among these rules was the banning of "talking drums," an African cultural tradition during slave gatherings. Designated a National Historic Landmark in 1974.

## PINEWOOD

**MILLFORD PLANTATION** Outstanding example of pre–Civil War Southern plantation architecture. Located in Sumter County in central South Carolina, the main house was built between 1839 and 1841 by Governor John Laurence Manning and his wife, Susan Francis Hampton Manning. It has been called "the finest Greek Revival house in South Carolina." The central structure is fronted by a portico, or open porch, with six large Corinthian columns. Verandas connect

### ❖ PINEWOOD ❖

- Located in central South Carolina
- The population of Pinewood is about 600.
- An agricultural village, Pinewood produces livestock, tobacco, cotton, grain, and peanuts.

the dwelling area with side structures on either wing. The mansion was once the heart of a flourishing cotton plantation. Its beautifully landscaped grounds include a stable and a springhouse (for cool food storage).

Millford Plantation was bought and restored by the prominent financier and art collector Richard Jenrette, who has preserved several other historically important houses. The Millford mansion contains a fine collection of nineteenth-century art and furniture. Designated a National Historic Landmark in 1973.

---

## MORE SITES

### COWPENS NATIONAL BATTLEFIELD

Site north of present-day Spartanburg, where an important battle in the American Revolution was fought on January 17, 1781. The victory by colonial forces helped turn the tide against the British campaign in the South. Became a National Battlefield in 1972.

### CHARLESTON HISTORIC DISTRICT

Location on the Charleston waterfront, the site where the city was founded in 1670. A large number of the early buildings still exist. The city passed a preservation law in 1931, making it one of the first historic sites in the nation. Designated a National Historical Landmark in 1960.

# SOUTH DAKOTA

## DEADWOOD

### DEADWOOD HISTORIC DISTRICT

Gold-mining town in the Black Hills that preserves the atmosphere of the Wild West. The town developed after the discovery of gold in 1874. It began as a tent-and-cabin settlement for miners and grew to a population of 2,000 by 1876. Fires ravaged the town in the early years. It took its name from the fallen, charred timbers that piled up everywhere. In its heyday, Deadwood was the home of frontier legends Wild Bill Hickock, Calamity Jane, and Deadwood Dick. Many of these figures are buried in a cemetery on Mount Moriah outside town.

The main street in Deadwood still has several well preserved original buildings. Among the attractions is the saloon claiming to be the one where Hickock was shot

### ❖ DEADWOOD ❖

- Settled in 1876 after gold was discovered in Deadwood Gulch
- Located in the Black Hills of western South Dakota, which is bordered by North Dakota, Minnesota, Iowa, Nebraska, Wyoming, and Montana
- Site of the graves of Wild Bill Hickock and Calamity Jane
- A tourist town with legalized gambling, Deadwood retains many characteristics of the Wild West.

in the back by "Crooked Nose Jack" McCall during a poker game on August 2, 1876. (The cards Hickock was holding at the time, aces and eights, became known as the "dead man's hand.") The Adams Museum displays artifacts of the town's history. The Days of '76 celebration, held every summer, recalls frontier life and the gold rush. Designated a National Historic Landmark in 1961.

Today, tourism—not gold—is the attraction in Deadwood, pictured above.

ernment officials sent in troops to arrest tribal leaders. Chief Sitting Bull was killed, and Sioux villagers led by Chief Big Foot fled their encampment on the Cheyenne River. Federal troops rounded up the Native Americans and moved them to a camp at Wounded Knee Creek. A shot was fired as the troops tried to disarm the Lakota. In the ensuing battle, the cavalry killed nearly 300 Lakota, about half of them women and children. Twenty-five soldiers were killed. Designated a National Historic Landmark in 1965.

## PINE RIDGE INDIAN RESERVATION

**WOUNDED KNEE BATTLEFIELD** Site of a massacre of the Lakota by the United States 7th Cavalry on December 29, 1890. It was the last major clash between Native Americans and whites in the United States. To later generations of Native Americans, it became a symbol of the violence and injustice inflicted on their people by the government. To many historians, it marks the passing of the American frontier.

The cause of the incident was a result of white men's fear of a new native religion called the Ghost Dance. Rituals and songs were based on the belief that the buffalo and Native American dead would be revived, that the whites would disappear, and that native lands would be returned to the Lakota people. Fearing an uprising, gov-

### ❖ PINE RIDGE INDIAN RESERVATION ❖

- Created in 1878
- The reservation covers about 2 million square miles (5,180,000 square kilometers).
- The site of the first wholly owned Native American radio station in the United States

## MORE SITES

**MOUNT RUSHMORE NATIONAL MEMORIAL** Gigantic sculptures of the heads of four American presidents—George Washington, Thomas Jefferson, Abraham

Lincoln, and Theodore Roosevelt—carved in the granite of a 5,725-foot (1,745-meter) mountain face in south-western South Dakota. Each head measures about 60 feet (18 meters) from chin to forehead. Sculptor Gutzon Borglum designed the work and oversaw construction, which was completed in 1941. Became a National Memorial in 1925.

**CROW CREEK SITE** Located near the town of Chamberlain, a large prehistoric Native American settlement. The site holds artifacts from two diffeent groups. The older group, the Crow Creek people from about A.D. 1100–1150, were attacked and conquered around A.D. 1325. Later, the Wolf Creek people lived on the same site from about A.D. 1400 to 1550. Designated a National Historic Landmark in 1964.

# TENNESSEE

## JAMESTOWN

**ALVIN CULLOM YORK FARM** Home of the World War I hero known as Sergeant York, from 1922 to his death in 1964. York enlisted in the army in 1917. He won his fame as an infantry corporal in the Battle of the Argonne Forest in northeastern France on October 8, 1918. A superb marksman, York led his men in the capture of a German machine-gun nest, killing 25 of the enemy. Acting almost

❖ JAMESTOWN ❖

- Founded in 1827
- Located in a hilly region of northern Tennessee, which is bordered by Kentucky, Virginia, North Carolina, Georgia, Alabama, Mississippi, Arkansas, and Missouri
- Natural fuels, timber, and livestock are the mainstays of the local economy.

entirely on his own, he then took 132 prisoners and 35 machine guns.

For his bravery, York was promoted to sergeant and awarded numerous decorations, including the Congressional Medal of Honor. His life and exploits were dramatized in the 1941 movie *Sergeant York*, starring Gary Cooper. The state of Tennessee gave him the 396-acre (160-hectare) farm that became his home. Designated a National Historic Landmark in 1976.

## NASHVILLE

**THE HERMITAGE** Stately plantation house east of Nashville that was the residence of Andrew Jackson (1767–1845), a military hero in the War of 1812 and the seventh president of the United States. Andrew and Rachel Jackson purchased the property in 1804. He called it home until his death 41 years later.

Jackson was born and reared on the SOUTH CAROLINA frontier. He moved to Nashville as a young man, where he began his career as a lawyer. He bought the farm after serving as a U.S. congressman, senator, and state court judge. For their first 17 years there, Andrew and Rachel Jackson lived in a log house. Jackson dedicated himself to growing cotton and raising horses.

Between 1819 and 1821, the Jacksons built a large brick house on the property. This would later be called the First Hermitage. By the end of his second term as president in 1837, Jackson had enlarged and remodeled it twice, creating the mansion that stands today. The farm grew to nearly 1,000 acres (400 hectares). Meanwhile, Rachel had died in 1828, and Jackson had a domed pavilion built over her grave. During his years as president, Jackson visited the Hermitage often. He spent his retirement years there and was buried beside his wife in the flower garden.

The Hermitage mansion is Greek Revival in style, with columned porticos, or porches, in the front and rear. The

The Hermitage, President Andrew Jackson's stately mansion, is a favorite tourist destination. Jackson and his wife, Rachel, are buried on the estate.

interior features a mantelpiece made of hickory sticks, a reminder of the owner's nickname—"Old Hickory." The house has been restored inside and out. Designated a National Historic Landmark in 1960.

## ❖ N A S H V I L L E ❖

- 🌿 Founded in 1779 as "Fort Nashborough" by James Robinson
- 🌿 A port of entry located on the Cumberland River in north-central Tennessee
- 🌿 State capital of Tennessee
- 🌿 An important Union base during the Civil War (1861–1865)
- 🌿 Called "Athens of the South" because it has many buildings of classical design
- 🌿 A center of the music recording industry, particularly country music

## MORE SITES

**GRACELAND** The Memphis mansion and burial site of rock 'n' roll superstar Elvis Presley (1935–1977). Now a museum housing memorabilia of the "King" and his career, Graceland continues to attract throngs of Elvis's fans. Listed in the National Register of Historic Places in 1991.

**TENNESSEE STATE CAPITOL** Located high on a hill in Nashville, Tennessee's State Capitol is designed in the Greek Revival style. Its porticos, or open porches, are modeled after the Erectheum, a building in Athens, Greece. Designed by architect William Strickland, it was built between 1845 and 1859. Designated a National Historic Landmark in 1971.

# TEXAS

## BEAUMONT

**LUCAS GUSHER SPINDLETOP OIL FIELD** Site of the first great oil strike in Texas and the birthplace of the modern petroleum industry. On January 10, 1901, a mining engineer, Anthony F. Lucas, struck a giant gusher, unleashing a geyser of oil that shot nearly 200 feet (60 meters)

### ❖ BEAUMONT ❖

- Incorporated in 1858
- Located on the Sabine-Naches waterway in southeastern Texas, which is bordered by Oklahoma, Arkansas, Louisiana, New Mexico, the Gulf of Mexico, and the Mexican states of Tamaulipas, Nuevo Leon, Coahuila, and Chihuahua
- Part of a large petrochemical and industrial complex called the "Golden Triangle," together with Port Arthur and Port Orange

The oil industry boomed after Anthony F. Lucas struck oil. Today, the site of the gusher is marked with a single oil derrick and pump.

in the air. It continued spewing at a rate of 75,000 barrels per day before being capped a week later. The area around Spindletop Hill, located just north of the Gulf of Mexico, proved to be one of the richest oil fields ever discovered. Within one year, nearly 300 wells were opened, and more than 500 oil companies were created. Refineries were built and an industry was born.

The output of the Spindletop field began to decline as early as 1903 and soon neared depletion. Deeper drilling in the 1920s tapped new reserves, and the field flourished until the 1950s. Sulfur mining then took over as the leading industry. In the meantime, vast oil deposits had been opened along the Texas and LOUISIANA coast. Today, a monument, pump, and replica of the original derrick—the wooden tower that stands over the well, used for hoisting and pumping—mark the site of the Lucas strike. Designated a National Historic Landmark in 1966.

## HOUSTON

### APOLLO MISSION CONTROL CENTER

Also known as the Johnson Space Center, where planning, training, and ground control for the U.S. space program are conducted. An installation of the National Aeronautics and Space Administration (NASA), the Johnson Space Center has directed the crewed Gemini space flights, Apollo Moon missions, space shuttle, and International Space Station projects. In July 1969, engineers and space scientists at the Mission Control Center monitored and guided the historic Moon-landing mission of *Apollo 11*.

Plans for the Houston facility were announced in 1961, shortly after President John Kennedy declared the goal of landing a man on the Moon. Completed in 1964, it was originally called the Manned Spacecraft Center. In 1973, it was renamed the Lyndon B. Johnson Space Flight Center after the late president and Texas native. Other personnel and facilities at the Johnson Space Flight Center are dedicated to designing, building, and

❖ HOUSTON ❖

- Founded in 1836 by brothers J.K. and A.C. Allen
- A deep-water port and port of entry located on the Houston Ship Channel in southeastern Texas
- Named for Sam Houston, president of the Republic of Texas (1836–1838, 1841–1844)
- Served as capital of the Republic of Texas (1837–1839)
- The largest city in Texas, the South, and the Southeast

testing spacecraft and special equipment; training astronauts; conducting scientific and medical research; and coordinating the efforts of private companies and foreign nations that participate in the space program. Designated a National Historic Landmark in 1985. *See also* FLORIDA.

## KINGSVILLE

### KING RANCH The largest and most famous ranch in the United States, covering nearly 1,000,000 acres (400,000 hectares) across four counties in southern Texas. It is larger than the entire state of RHODE ISLAND. Captain Richard King (1824–1885), a native of NEW YORK who had moved to the Rio Grande Valley to serve in the Mexican War, began the ranch with the purchase of 75,000 acres (30,375 hectares) during the years of 1853 and 1854.

- The town was founded in 1904, but the area's history goes back to 1853.
- Located in South Texas
- The Kingsville Naval Air Station is one of the best-known jet-pilot training schools in the nation.

King and his wife Henrietta pursued their dreams of raising prime livestock and taming the desert. They acquired and developed more land, amassing a fortune by shipping cattle, sheep, goats, and horses to the north. Investments in fencing, packinghouses, railroad lines, and other facilities helped shape the ranching and livestock industry of the West. After Captain King's death in 1885, Henrietta and her business manager, Robert J. Kleberg, continued to acquire land and contributed heavily to the construction of churches, libraries, and schools in the town of Kingsville. Between 1912 and 1915, she built a lavish Spanish-style mansion as a family residence and stopping place for travelers. Among the many livestock innovations at the King Ranch was the breeding of the Santa Gertrudis line, now a common beef cattle, in 1920.

The King Ranch today is a diversified ranching and agricultural corporation. Descendants of Captain King still play a major role in managing the business. The wealth of wildlife on the land attracts hunters and birdwatchers throughout the year. A museum was opened in 1990. Designated a National Historic Landmark in 1961.

## SAN ANTONIO

**THE ALAMO** Former Spanish mission that was the site of a historic battle in the Texas Revolution in February and March of 1836. The defense of the Alamo by a small band of mostly Texans against an overwhelming Mexican army made it a symbol of, and inspiration for, the cause of Texas independence. "Remember the Alamo!" became the battle cry of the revolution. The site became known as the "Cradle of Texas Liberty."

**HISTORY** The Alamo was founded in 1718 as the Mission San Antonio de Valero. Built by Franciscan priests, it was one of the first settlements in what would

- Founded in 1718, with the establishment of a Franciscan mission—San Antonio de Valero, or "The Alamo"—and a Spanish fort—the presidio of San Antonio de Bexar
- Located at the head of the San Antonio River in south-central Texas
- A port of entry and one of the nation's largest military centers
- San Antonio's tree-lined river, large Mexican quarter, Franciscan missions, and warm climate attract thousands of tourists each year
- Captured by Texans during the Texas Revolution (1835) and site of the Mexican attack on the Alamo (1836)

become the city of San Antonio. In the 1790s, the building was converted into a military fortress and barracks. It was named "Alamo" after the cottonwood trees (*alamos* in Spanish) that grew in the area.

The chain of events that made the Alamo famous began on February 24, 1836. American settlers had launched the fight for independence against Mexico the previous October. The Alamo served as Mexican military headquarters until December, when Texan forces attacked and captured it. The Mexican dictator and general, Antonio López de Santa Anna then led an army of several thousand men to the site and laid siege. The compound consisted of stone walls surrounding a courtyard and church. Defending it were about 185 or 190 troops, commanded by

After Texas won its independence in 1836, the Alamo was returned to the Catholic Church. Beginning in 1845, after Texas became part of the United States, the army leased the Alamo from Church authorities until the State of Texas finally bought the Alamo in 1883.

## ★ PROFILE ★
### SAMUEL HOUSTON

One of the most colorful figures of the American frontier, Samuel Houston (1793–1863) was the commanding general of Texas armed forces in the revolution against Mexico (1835–1836) and the first president of the Republic of Texas (1836–1838 and 1841–1844). After Texas was annexed by the United States in 1845, he served as U.S. senator (1846–1859) and governor (1859–1861). He was removed as governor for refusing to support secession from the Union. Houston was raised in TENNESSEE, where he studied law, was elected twice to the U.S. Congress (1823–1827), and also served as governor (1828–1832).

Colonel William B. Travis. The troops included the famous Jim Bowie and Davy Crockett.

For nearly two weeks, the Texans defended the Alamo against cannon fire and repeated attacks. Finally, on March 6, Mexican troops succeeded in scaling the walls and taking the fortress. The Mexicans suffered more than 1,500 casualties. Those losses, the delay of Santa Anna's invasion, and the inspiration to the Texan cause contributed to Mexico's final defeat six weeks later.

TODAY The walls of the mission church, the only remaining section, stand in a landscaped park in downtown San Antonio. A marble plaque lists the names of the defenders. The Daughters of the Republic of Texas maintains the site as a shrine to the defenders, with a museum dedicated to Texas history. Designated a National Historic Landmark in 1960.

---

## MORE SITES

**DEALEY PLAZA HISTORIC DISTRICT** A small landscaped park in downtown Dallas through which President John F. Kennedy was riding in a motorcade when he was assassinated on November 22, 1963. As his motorcade drove past, shots were fired from the nearby Texas School Book Depository Building. Designated a National Historic Landmark in 1993.

**FORT SAM HOUSTON** United States Army post in San Antonio. Built in 1879, it became the principal training and supply center in the Southwest. Theodore Roosevelt's Rough Riders trained there in 1898. A 1910 flight by Lieutenant Benjamin Foulois marked the birth of U.S. military aviation. Still active, "Fort Sam" today covers 54 square miles (140 square kilometers). Designated a National Historic Landmark in 1975.

# UTAH

## BRIGHAM CITY

**GOLDEN SPIKE NATIONAL HISTORIC SITE** Spot at Promontory Point, 31 miles (49.8 kilometers) west of Brigham City, where the nation's first transcontinental railroad was completed on May 10, 1869. It was here that tracks of the Central Pacific Railroad (laid eastward from Sacramento, CALIFORNIA) met those of the Union Pacific Railroad (laid westward from Omaha, NEBRASKA). Travel time from the Missouri River to the Pacific Coast was reduced from about six months to six days. Chinese and Irish immigrants constructed most of the 1,800 miles (2,900 kilometers) of new track. The meeting of the two lines at Promontory Point was marked by a colorful ceremony that included the driving of a golden spike. A stone monument marks the site. Established as a National Historic Site in 1957.

### ❖ BRIGHAM CITY ❖

- Founded as "Box Elder" in 1851
- Located in northern Utah, which is bordered by Idaho, Wyoming, Colorado, Arizona, New Mexico, and Nevada
- Renamed in 1856 to honor Brigham Young, a Mormon spiritual leader and governor of Utah Territory (1849–1857)

## SALT LAKE CITY

**TEMPLE SQUARE** Ten-acre (4-hectare) area in Salt Lake City that is sacred to members of the Church of Jesus Christ of Latter-day Saints (Mormons). "Here will be the temple of our God," declared leader Brigham Young after arriving in the Utah desert in July 1847. At the heart of the square—and

### BRIGHAM YOUNG

**T**he second president (after Joseph Smith) of the Church of Jesus Christ of Latter-day Saints, Brigham Young (1801–1877) led followers of the Church on their migration from the Midwest to establish a home in the valley of the Great Salt Lake in 1847. The Church prospered under his direction, and the site he chose for its center became the city of Salt Lake City. Pioneering parties he sent out from there founded more than 350 other communities in the West. Young also served as the first governor of the Utah Territory from 1849 to 1857.

Temple Square is the center of Salt Lake City. The square is owned and operated by the Church of Jesus Christ of Latter-day Saints.

the Mormon faith—stands the massive granite Temple, built between 1853 and 1893. Also located within the square are the Tabernacle (1863–1867), home of the world-famous Mormon Tabernacle Choir, and the Assembly Hall (1877–1882). The temple is open only to Church members; the square and tabernacle are open to the general public. Designated a National Historic Landmark in 1964.

### ❖ SALT LAKE CITY ❖

- Founded by Mormon pioneers in 1847
- Located in north-central Utah
- Largest city and state capital of Utah
- Site of the 2002 Olympic games

## WENDOVER

**DANGER CAVE** Site on the western edge of the Great Salt Lake region (known as the Great Basin) where excavations have provided evidence of continuous human life for more than 10,000 years (9,000 B.C. to A.D. 1400). Dry conditions in the cave preserved a variety of remains and artifacts, including human and animal skeletons, tools, baskets, items of clothing, and ornaments.

Archaeologists have identified at least five layers of deposits, each associated with a different phase of life in the region. Explorations began in 1949, and discoveries have enabled scientists to trace changes in lifestyle and culture through the millennia. The inhabitants of the cave were hunter-gatherers whose tools advanced from stone points and spears to bows and arrows. The earliest occupants belonged to Paleo-Indian cultures, roving game hunters who were among the first native peoples of North America. Later occupants represented phases of the Desert Archaic culture. These prehistoric humans lived in family groups of between 25 and 30 and survived on meat, nuts, and seeds. Designated a National Historic Landmark in 1961.

## MORE SITES

**BINGHAM CANYON COPPER MINE** The world's first open-pit copper mine, started in 1904 near Salt Lake City. The largest human excavation on earth, it now measures more than 2.5 miles (4 kilometers) wide and one-half mile (0.8 kilometers) deep. It remains the nation's single largest source of copper. Designated a National Historic Landmark in 1966.

**OLD CITY HALL** Located in Salt Lake City, a redstone building that served as both the capital of the Utah Territory and city hall until 1894. Also known as Council Hall, it was built between 1864 and 1866. In 1961, the structure was taken down and moved to the grounds of the present-day Utah State Capitol. Designated a National Historic Landmark in 1975.

# VERMONT

**ROKEBY** Located in the town of Ferris-burgh, home to four generations of Quakers—the Robinsons—and a major stop on the Underground Railroad. The Robinson family first settled the farm in the 1790s.

Rokeby is one of the best-preserved Underground Railroad sites in the nation. The abolitionist Robinson family kept detailed records about the runaways who stopped at Rokeby on their way to Canada. Many of the furnishings in the house are original and provide a look into the rural past.

Today, this 90-acre (36.4-hectare) site is a museum and is open year round for a variety of tours. Designated a National Historic Landmark in 1997. *See also* ILLINOIS.

The Rokeby granary combines the functions of both a granary—for storage—and a corncrib—for feeding animals—into one farm building. Unlike other farm structures, the granary was built off the ground on stone posts to discourage rodents from eating the grains stored inside.

### ❖ FERRISBURGH ❖

- Settled by Europeans in 1769
- A town of about 2,400 people in northern Vermont, which is bordered by New Hampshire, Massachusetts, New York, and the Canadian province of Quebec
- Named for the surveyors of the area, Benjamin and David Ferris

## ORWELL

**MOUNT INDEPENDENCE** Site of one of the most important early Revolutionary War forts in Vermont, located across a lake from Fort Ticonderoga. Colonial troops began to fortify the area in June 1776 to keep the British troops in Canada from reaching the Hudson River, thus separating the New England colonies from the others. By early July 1777, however, the Americans left the site as British General John Burgoyne overwhelmed the area. American troops fought Burgoyne at Bennington, Vermont, and later that year won a great victory at Saratoga, NEW YORK.

After hearing of the American victory at Saratoga, the remaining British troops at Mount Independence burned the site.

Mount Independence is open to the public, and visitors can hike scenic trails and explore the remains of the barracks, the hospital, and blockhouses. Designated a National Historic Landmark in 1972.

### ❖ ORWELL ❖

- A town settled in 1771
- Site of Mount Independence, which is named for the Declaration of Independence

---

### MORE SITES

**SHELBURNE FARMS** Located on the shore of Lake Champlain in northwestern Vermont, a 14,000-acre (5,665.5-hectare) working farm, environmental education center, and country inn. Designated a National Historic Landmark in 2001.

**CALVIN COOLIDGE HOMESTEAD DISTRICT** The site where Calvin Coolidge was born in 1872 and later sworn in as the thirtieth president of the United States (1923–1929). Today, much of the village of Plymouth Notch is owned by the state of Vermont and is open to the public. Six generations of Coolidges, including the former president, are buried in a small cemetery near the village. Designated a National Historic Landmark in 1965.

# VIRGINIA

## APPOMATTOX

**APPOMATTOX COURT HOUSE NATIONAL HISTORIC PARK** Village in southern Virginia where, on April 9, 1865, Confederate general Robert E. Lee surrendered to Union general Ulysses S. Grant, effectively ending the Civil War. The signing of the surrender papers took place in the parlor of Wilmer McLean's farmhouse. Scattered Confederate units held out for a few more weeks, but Lee's surrender of the Army of Northern Virginia signaled the defeat of the Confederacy. Grant provided rations for Lee's starving troops and ordered that they be allowed to return home unharmed.

The surrender at Appomattox followed a string of devastating losses for the Army of Northern Virginia. For months, the army had been surrounded at Petersburg, critical to its defense of the Confederate capital of Richmond. Lee's army managed to

### ❖ APPOMATTOX ❖

- The area is noted on a 1612 map drawn by explorer Captain John Smith.
- County boundaries established in 1845
- A small town with a population of about 1,700, located in central Virginia
- Site of Confederate general Robert E. Lee's surrender to Union general Ulysses S. Grant in 1865

escape in early April, hoping to link up with other Confederate forces to the south. Led by General Philip Sheridan, Union troops blocked the retreat and inflicted heavy casualties. After a final skirmish at Appomattox Court House on April 8, Lee's once vast army numbered only 9,000. There was no choice but to surrender. The remaining Confederate soldiers laid down their weapons, and Lee bid them farewell.

Confederate general Lee surrendered to Union general Grant in the front parlor of McLean's farmhouse.

The McLean farmhouse, dismantled in 1893, was later rebuilt on the same site using much of the original material. Other buildings restored to their 1865 appearance and open to visitors include the courthouse (now a museum), county jail, general store, and private homes. Designated a National Historic Park in 1954. *See also* PENNSYLVANIA.

## CHARLOTTESVILLE

**MONTICELLO** Beloved mountaintop residence and plantation of Thomas Jefferson for more than 50 years. Monticello, meaning "little mountain" in Italian, was virtually a lifelong project for Jefferson. He designed the house and grounds, and he was involved in every detail of construction and renovation. The red-brick domed house—an original blend of Roman, French, and Palladian styles—is one of the most admired works in American architecture. Since 1939, it has

### ❖ CHARLOTTESVILLE ❖

- Founded in 1762
- Located in central Virginia on the Rivanna River
- Named after Queen Charlotte, King George III's young bride
- Site of the homes of Thomas Jefferson and James Monroe, and the birthplaces of explorers Meriwether Lewis and George Rogers Clark

appeared on the reverse, or "tails," side of the nickel coin.

HISTORY Jefferson played on his father's land as a boy and inherited several thousand acres at age 21. He began building his home

★ PROFILE ★

## THOMAS JEFFERSON

A towering figure in the founding of the United States, Jefferson (1743–1826) was also noted as a scholar, naturalist, and architect. As a colonial patriot, he was the author of the Declaration of Independence, a revolutionary leader in the Virginia legislature, wartime governor, key member of the Continental Congress, and minister to France. In the new republic, he served as secretary of state to George Washington and as vice president to John Adams, and he served two terms as president (1801–1809). As chief executive, he was responsible for the Louisiana Purchase of 1803 and the Lewis and Clark expedition to explore the West. He designed and built his Monticello home, as well as the state capitol in Richmond, and he was the founder and architect of the University of Virginia at Charlottesville.

in 1769 but began redesigning it after returning from France, where he had served as colonial minister, in 1789. Construction on the new Monticello commenced in 1796 and continued until 1817, and Jefferson made additions until his death in 1826. The new house featured a dome, columnar porticos, or porches, at the front and rear, and many rooms of different shape.

The house was the center of a working plantation that grew to 5,000 acres

(2,000 hectares) and included four adjacent farms. Jefferson began by planting tobacco, later turning to wheat, corn, potatoes, and grains. The grounds also included a large botanical garden, in which he grew more than 400 different fruits and vegetables. Jefferson experimented with a variety of techniques to raise better crops. Farm work and household chores were carried out by as many as 135 slaves, who lived in quarters near the main house. Jefferson and members of his family are buried in a cemetery at the western edge of the grounds.

TODAY Visitors to Monticello are attracted by its historical interest, architectural beauty, and scenic views. Especially fascinating are the many artifacts, memorabilia, and Jeffersonian inventions collected in the house. Recent excavations on the estate have provided insights into slave life and the workings of the plantation. Designated a National Historic Landmark in 1960.

**UNIVERSITY OF VIRGINIA HISTORIC DISTRICT** The original grounds and buildings of Virginia's state university, founded by Thomas Jefferson in 1817. Jefferson also designed the buildings, laid out the campus, established the course of study, and hired the first professors. The most prominent building is the domed Rotunda, which opened in 1826 and had the university library located on the second floor. South of the Rotunda lies the "Lawn," a broad tree-lined space that has, on two sides, ten pavilions for the faculty and teaching. In between is a dormitory for students. Colonnades—covered passageways supported by columns—connect the complex. Behind the Lawn lie gardens with curving walls and an outer row of dormitory rooms.

HISTORY Jefferson had long dreamed of a public university, independent of organized religion, that would be "the most eminent in the United States." His enlistment of support from the Virginia legislature, design of the campus, and leadership of the new institution were his greatest passions after leaving the White House in 1809. Originally chartered as Central College in 1817, it became the University of Virginia in 1819. The school was opened to students in 1825, when Jefferson was 82 years old.

The domed Rotunda, modeled after the Pantheon in Rome, served as a Confederate military hospital during the Civil War (1861–1865). It was severely damaged by fire in 1895, but it was rebuilt within three years. It remains the most familiar landmark on the university campus.

TODAY The University of Virginia is one of the nation's foremost public institutions of higher learning. It offers a full range of undergraduate, graduate, and professional

Thomas Jefferson designed the University of Virginia's Rotunda to reflect his belief that a university should be a community of scholars. The Rotunda originally served as a library and meeting place.

degrees—including law and medicine. The academic community consists of nearly 20,000 enrolled students and more than 1,900 faculty members. Jefferson's original buildings continue to be used for faculty housing, classrooms, and offices. Designated a National Historic Landmark in 1971.

## MOUNT VERNON

MOUNT VERNON The home of George Washington, a 500-acre (200-hectare) estate overlooking the Potomac River. Washington first moved to the property at age 11, in 1743. He died there on December 14, 1799. The house was built in stages over several decades. It was

## ❖ MOUNT VERNON ❖

- Located about 7 miles (11.2 kilometers) south of Alexandria in northern Virginia, which is bordered by West Virginia, Maryland, North Carolina, Tennessee, Kentucky, the Chesapeake Bay, and the Atlantic Ocean
- Settled by English settlers in the 1600s

considered a national shrine after the American Revolution (1775–1783) and remains a popular tourist site today.

HISTORY Washington's great-grandfather, Colonel John Washington, acquired the property in 1674. The land passed to Lawrence Washington, George's half-brother, in 1743. Young George moved there with him. Lawrence named the estate in honor of his commanding officer in the British navy, Admiral Edward Vernon. In 1754, shortly after Lawrence died, George leased the property from his widow. He inherited it from her eight years later.

The main residence in 1754 was a four-room cottage. This would form the core of Washington's Mansion House. In 1757 to 1758, after serving in the French and Indian War, he added a second floor, refinished the outside walls, and remodeled the interior. In the 1780s, after returning from the Revolutionary War, he expanded the house, added the now-familiar pillared porch, and built several outbuildings. By 1787, Mount Vernon had assumed its present appearance.

During the years before and after his presidency, Washington grew crops—tobacco, wheat, and grain—and bred horses and hunting dogs, and entertained guests at Mount Vernon. At its peak, the plantation covered 8,000 acres (3,240 hectares). As many as 200 enslaved African Americans worked the fields and served the residence.

TODAY The Mount Vernon Ladies Association purchased the estate in 1858. The organization has restored and maintained the property as it appeared in Washington's later years. The house is filled with family memorabilia and historical artifacts, providing a vivid portrait of Washington's life. The tombs of George and Martha Washington are located on the grounds. Designated a National Historic Landmark in 1960. *See also* MARYLAND, NEW JERSEY, PENNSYLVANIA, and WASHINGTON, D.C.

---

## MORE SITES

**THE PENTAGON** Headquarters of the United States Department of Defense, Army, Navy, and Air Force, located in Arlington across the Potomac River from WASHINGTON, D.C. The world's largest office facility, it consists of five concentric, five-sided, buildings, each five stories, joined by corridors. It was completed in January 1943 after only 16 months of construction. Designated a National Historic Landmark in 1992.

## WILLIAMSBURG HISTORIC DISTRICT

The colonial capital of Virginia from 1698 to 1779 and a major historic preservation site. Funded by John D. Rockefeller, the restoration began in 1929 and now includes more than 500 buildings. Visitors to Colonial Williamsburg enjoy special displays and demonstrations on the history, culture, and everyday life of pre-Revolutionary America. Designated a National Historic Landmark in 1960.

# WASHINGTON

## BREMERTON

### PUGET SOUND NAVAL SHIPYARD

The primary repair center for the United States Navy during World War II (1939–1945). The Bremerton shipyard, located across Puget Sound from Seattle, played a vital role in restoring the American fleet after the devastating 1941 attack on Pearl Harbor in HAWAII. Five of the eight battleships damaged in the bombing were repaired at the facility and returned to service. Workers at the shipyard restored, built, or refitted some 400 warships between 1941 and 1945.

The original naval station was founded in 1891 and designated Navy Yard Puget Sound in 1901. It was heavily involved in ship construction during World War I (1914–1918), later shifting its emphasis to repair. The facility was

### ❖ BREMERTON ❖

🔹 Established in 1891 when the area was selected as the site of the Puget Sound Naval Shipyard

🔹 Located in northwest Washington, which is bordered by Idaho, Oregon, the Canadian province of British Columbia, and the Pacific Ocean

🔹 Gateway to the Olympic Peninsula, with easy access to the Cascade and Olympic mountains

Puget Sound Naval Shipyard was home to the USS *Missouri* (center), the battleship that was the site of the September 2, 1945, Japanese surrender ceremony that ended World War II. In 1998, it was moved to Pearl Harbor, Hawaii, and became a memorial.

renamed Puget Sound Naval Shipyard after World War II. Since then, efforts have focused on the modernization of aircraft carriers, on the activation of ships for the Korean War (1950–1953), on the construction of guided-missile frigates, and on the deactivation and recycling of nuclear-powered vessels. It remains an important maintenance facility for the United States Navy. Designated a National Historic Landmark in 1992.

## CHINOOK

**CHINOOK POINT** Site at the entrance to the Columbia River where the American sea captain and fur trader Robert Gray landed in May 1792. According to international law at the time, entering the mouth of a river gave the discoverer's country sovereignty, or posses-

### ❖ CHINOOK ❖

- The area may have had settlers as early as the 1840s
- A village located in southwest Washington
- The manufacturing of fresh and frozen seafood is the mainstay of the local economy.

sion, over the water and surrounding land. By sailing his ship, the *Columbia*, upriver to Chinook Point, Gray gave the United States a claim to the Pacific Northwest. Great Britain, whose ships had also explored the area, contested the American claim, but the Oregon Treaty of 1846 finally resolved the matter. Designated a National Historic Landmark in 1961.

## MORE SITES

**PORT TOWNSEND** City on Puget Sound that flourished as a port, lumbering center, and customs station from the 1850s to 1880s. The city features ornate Victorian houses and public buildings of architectural distinction. Designated as a National Historic Landmark in 1977.

**PORT GAMBLE HISTORIC DISTRICT** One of the earliest lumber-producing centers on the Pacific coast. In 1853, Captain William C. Talbot built a lumber camp and sawmill on the forested Kitsap Peninsula, which quickly became an important forestry company. Although the mill closed in 1997, the town remains a model of a company town of the mid-1800s. Designated a National Historic Landmark in 1966.

# WEST VIRGINIA

## WHEELING

### WHEELING SUSPENSION BRIDGE

The first bridge to cross the Ohio River, built in 1849. At 1,010 feet (308 meters), it was the longest suspension bridge in the world at the time. Construction of the bridge contributed to the importance of Wheeling as an industrial community, shipping center, and railroad junction.

The Wheeling Bridge was designed by Charles Ellet, Jr. (1810–1862), a civil engineer known for building the first suspension bridges in the United States. The span at Wheeling was suspended by six wire cables that hung between two towers. After suffering severe storm damage in 1854, the structure was rebuilt in 1860. Stronger cables were added in 1871 and 1872 by Washington Roebling, who is best known for his work on the Brooklyn Bridge in NEW YORK. The Wheeling Bridge is the oldest cable suspension bridge still in use in the United States today. Designated a National Historic Landmark in 1975.

## ❖ WHEELING ❖

- Settled in 1769
- Located on the Ohio River in northern West Virginia, which is bordered by Pennsylvania, Maryland, Virginia, Kentucky, and Ohio
- Site of Fort Henry, which was attacked by Native Americans in 1777, 1781, and 1782
- An important trading post until the 1850s and center of pro-Union activity during the Civil War (1861–1865)
- Served as capital of West Virginia (1863–1870 and 1875–1885)

## WHITE SULPHUR SPRINGS

### THE GREENBRIER

One of the oldest and most luxurious resort hotels in the United States. It is located in the Allegheny mountain town of White Sulphur Springs, long popular for its natural spa

One of the most luxurious resorts in the country, the Greenbrier is also famous for the underground bunker that was top secret until 1992. The government code word for the bunker was "Project Greek Island."

- Settled in 1750
- Located in the Allegheny Mountains in southeastern West Virginia
- A well-known mineral springs resort since the early 1830s

waters. The first inn appeared at the site in 1780. Wealthy Southerners began building vacation cottages, now used as guesthouses, in the decades that followed. A large hotel called the White Sulphur, completed in 1858, attracted the upper crust of Southern society in the years before the Civil War.

The stately white-columned main building of today was built between 1910 and 1913, when the hotel was renamed the Greenbrier. Enlarged and renovated several times over the decades, it served as a United States Army hospital during World War II (1939–1945) and was reopened in grand style in 1948. The large West Virginia Wing was added in 1960. Today, the Greenbrier is a 6,500-acre (2,600-hectare) estate with 739 rooms and suites, dining halls and restaurants, conference halls, three golf courses, and a wide variety of other recreational facilities.

The historical interest of the Greenbrier took on a new dimension in the early 1990s, when it was revealed that the U.S. government had maintained a top-secret bunker complex under the west wing. Dating to 1960, the underground facility was built to accommodate American congressional representatives and senators in the event of nuclear attack during the cold war—a prolonged period of tension between the United States and Soviet Union after World War II. The bunker is now open to visitors. Designated a National Historic Landmark in 1990.

## MORE SITES

**ELKINS COAL AND COKE COMPANY HISTORIC DISTRICT** A large complex of beehive coke ovens built between 1906 and 1919. These domed, brick blast-furnace ovens helped make the United States a leading producer of iron and steel in the early twentieth century. The facility closed in 1980. It is believed to have been the last facility of its kind. Designated a National Historic Landmark in 1983.

**WEST VIRGINIA INDEPENDENCE HALL** A Renaissance Revival building where the state of West Virginia was born. During the Civil War (1861–1865), the western counties of the state of Virginia opposed secession, or leaving the Union. Meeting in Wheeling, county leaders organized the Restored Government of Virginia, which was loyal to the United States. They then held a constitutional convention, and West Virginia became a separate state on June 20, 1863. The state bought and restored the building in the early 1960s. Today, it is a museum. Designated a National Historic Landmark in 1988.

# WISCONSIN

## RIPON

**LITTLE WHITE SCHOOLHOUSE** One-room schoolhouse where the Republican party was born on March 20, 1854. The creation of the party grew out of opposition to the extension of legalized slavery in the Kansas and Nebraska territories. Antislavery groups protested the proposed Kansas-Nebraska Act, then being debated in Congress. Enacted later that spring, this law repealed the Missouri Compromise of 1820, which had attempted to resolve the controversy over extending slavery into the territories. On a cold winter night in Ripon, 53 citizens met at the simple frame schoolhouse on Blackburn Street. Led by Alvan Earle Bovay, a local lawyer, the group voted to join a new political organization that would protect voters against the "Nebraska swindle." Bovay proposed that the new party be called Republican—the name formerly used by followers of Thomas Jefferson.

Many members of the Whig, Free Soil, and Democratic parties who opposed the spread of slavery joined the movement. Meetings were organized in other locations, more members were enlisted, and a new national party was born. In 1860, the Republican party elected its first U.S. president—Abraham Lincoln.

In 1954, the Republican party celebrated its one hundredth anniversary at

### ❖ RIPON ❖

- 🦋 Founded in 1844 by Socialist Fourierists—people inspired by the political ideas of French thinker Charles Fourier

- 🦋 An agricultural town located on Silver Creek in east-central Wisconsin, which is bordered by Michigan, Illinois, Iowa, Minnesota, and two Great Lakes—Michigan and Superior

The Little White School House was built in 1850. It quickly became a popular meeting place for Ripon, Wisconsin, citizens.

the Little White Schoolhouse. Today, it houses a small museum. Designated a National Historic Landmark in 1974.

## STURGEON BAY

**NAMUR HISTORIC DISTRICT** The largest Belgian settlement in the United States, located in Door, Brown, and Kewaunee counties on Wisconsin's eastern peninsula. The district includes 77 Belgian American properties on nearly 1,000 square miles (2,600 square kilometers) of agricultural land. It is named for the city in south-central Belgium that serves as the capital of Wallonia—one of that country's three self-governing regions.

Attracted by cheap, fertile land made available by the U.S. government, French-speaking Walloons began arriving in 1853. (The Walloons are an ethnic group from Wallonia. They have a unique cultural tradition and speak their own dialect of French.) More than 15,000 others followed the first handful of settlers over the next ten years. Most of the original wood buildings in the area were destroyed by fire in 1871. A few stone houses survived. Visitors can also see the many farmhouses, barns, granaries, and other farm structures built after 1871. The Namur district is still heavily reliant on agriculture. The ethnic flavor and beauty of the land attracts many tourists. Designated a National Historic Landmark in 1990.

❖ **S T U R G E O N   B A Y** ❖

- Incorporated in 1883
- Located at the head of Sturgeon Bay in northeastern Wisconsin
- A cherry-growing and resort center, Sturgeon Bay also contains large shipyards and manufactures electronic equipment and metal products.

## MORE SITES

**ROBERT M. LA FOLLETTE HOUSE** Suburban Madison home of the prominent reform politician for the last 20 years of his life. "Fighting Bob" La Follette (1855–1925) served as a U.S. congressman (1885–1891), governor of Wisconsin (1901–1906), and U.S. senator (1906–1925). He ran unsuccessfully for president on the Progressive party ticket in 1924. Today, the house is privately owned. Designated a National Historic Landmark in 1964.

**ASTOR FUR WAREHOUSE** A plain stone building built around 1828 that served as a fur-storage center in the first part of the nineteenth century. It is the only known original fur warehouse in the Upper Mississippi Valley, and played a key role in John Jacob Astor's American Fur Company. Its location near the town of Prairie du Chien on the Wisconsin River made it an important fur-trading post. Designated a National Historic Landmark in 1960.

# WYOMING

## GUERNSEY

**OREGON TRAIL RUTS** Wagon wheel ruts in east-central Wyoming that mark the famous overland route to the Western frontier. Preserved in sandstone on a ridge along the North Platte River, the ruts measure two to six feet (0.6 to 1.8 meters) deep.

Between 1841 and 1869, the Oregon Trail carried thousands of pioneers across the plains to the fertile farmlands of the Oregon Country. The route covered about 2,000 miles (3,200 kilometers) from Independence, MISSOURI, to the Pacific Northwest. Explorers, trappers, and missionaries opened the first stretches of the trail in the early 1800s. Completion of the transcontinental railroad in 1869 greatly reduced wagon traffic along the trail.

Located only a short distance from the wagon ruts is Register Cliff, another landmark of the old Oregon Trail. Thousands of pioneers inscribed their names in the soft sandstone, and several hundred are still visible today. The area was a popular stopping point for many wagon trains and includes a pioneer cemetery. Register Cliff and the trail ruts are in grassy terrain where the route emerges from the river valley and enters high plains to the west. Designated a National Historic Landmark in 1966. *See also* UTAH.

### ❖ GUERNSEY ❖

- A town located on the Platte River in southeast Wyoming, which is bordered by Montana, South Dakota, Nebraska, Colorado, Utah, and Idaho
- The town's population is about 1,500.
- Located about 97 miles (156 kilometers) from Cheyenne, the capital

## YELLOWSTONE NATIONAL PARK

**OLD FAITHFUL INN** Rustic hotel adjacent to the Old Faithful geyser and the most famous building in Yellowstone National Park. The inn was built during the bitter cold winter of 1903–1904. (It was so cold that workers kept their tools by a fire to keep them from shattering.) For nearly

The luxurious Old Faithful Inn was built on the site of the first hotel, which was called "the Shack" because visitors received splinters from the rough wood walls.

## ❖ YELLOWSTONE NATIONAL PARK ❖

- Located in the northwestern corner of Wyoming

- Became the country's first national park on March 1, 1872

- President Ulysses S. Grant signed the bill that authorized the park.

two decades, the site had been occupied by tent camps and shoddily constructed cabins. Seeking a first-class hotel for wealthy visitors, the Northern Pacific Railroad hired Robert Chambers Reamer to design an appropriate building. The Old Faithful Inn established a new style, called "rustic architecture," for national and state parks.

The inn was designed to fit the natural landscape and is distinguished by such features as railings constructed of naturally shaped logs and branches. The foundation, a large fireplace, and an 85-foot (26-meter) chimney were built of lava stone found in the park. The frame, walls, and ceilings were made of pinewood also gathered from the area. The building stands seven stories tall and features a lobby that rises the full height. Visitors to the 2.2-million-acre (890,000-hectare) national park still enjoy its superb accommodations. Designated a National Historic Landmark in 1987.

## MORE SITES

**FORT LARAMIE** Site in southeastern Wyoming established as a trading post by fur trappers in 1834, becoming an important supply depot for the Oregon Trail. Bought by the U.S. government in 1849, it became a military fort and the headquarters for campaigns against Native Americans. Fort Laramie was abandoned in 1890. Established as a National Historic Site in 1966.

**WYOMING STATE CAPITOL** An imposing three-and-a-half story sandstone building capped with a gold dome. Designed to resemble the United States Capitol in WASHINGTON, D.C., the building's cornerstone was laid in Cheyenne on May 18, 1887. Wyoming was the first state to grant women full voting rights. A statue of Esther Hobart Morris, who lobbied lawmakers to include women's suffrage in the new state constitution, stands in front of the main entrance. Listed on the National Register of Historic Places in 1987. *See also* GEORGIA.

# WASHINGTON, D.C.

WASHINGTON, D.C.

The Main Reading Room of the Library of Congress includes about 70,000 volumes of reference works.

**LIBRARY OF CONGRESS** Founded in 1800 to provide "such books as may be necessary for the use of Congress." In a law signed by President John Adams, Congress set aside $5,000 for the new library. Today, the main library is located in a Beaux Arts–inspired building designed in the 1870s and built in the 1890s. This building, one of three that the library occupies, is known as the Thomas Jefferson building.

HISTORY The Library of Congress was originally housed in the first Capitol—together with Congress and the Supreme Court. During the War of 1812, the British burned the Capitol and destroyed the library's collection of about 3,000 volumes. Congress purchased Thomas Jefferson's personal collection of books and papers—about 6,000 volumes—to rebuild the library in 1815. Congress paid $23,950 for Jefferson's library.

Twice more—in 1825 and 1851—fire destroyed part of the library's collection. In 1866, the Library of Congress expanded to include the Library of the Smithsonian Institution. In 1870, Congress determined that all copyrighted works in the United States should be kept in the Library of Congress. The library's rare book collections grew greatly in 1930 when Congress purchased more than 3,000 rare fifteenth-century books, including a Gutenberg Bible. As the

## ❖ WASHINGTON, D.C. ❖

- The nation's capital, Washington, D.C., is not part of any state.
- George Washington personally selected the location of the city.
- Located on the Potomac River between the states of Maryland and Virginia
- Congress first met in Washington, D.C. on November 17, 1800—even though construction of the capital city continued for many years.
- Benjamin Bannecker, a free African American, surveyed the land on which the city was built.

library continued to expand, two new buildings were added—the John Adams Annex in 1938 and the James Madison Building in 1981.

TODAY The library is now among the largest in the world. It houses millions of books and pamphlets, pieces of music, and photographs. Among its treasures is Thomas Jefferson's rough draft of the Declaration of Independence and James Madison's personal notes on the Constitutional Convention—the 1787 meeting in which the nation's founders wrote the United States Constitution. Although the library is open to the public, books may not be removed from the reading rooms. Designated a National Historic Landmark in 1965.

**OCTAGON HOUSE** Completed in 1800, a unique home designed by Dr. William Thornton, the architect who initially designed the United States Capitol. Although the name Octagon House implies that the structure has eight sides, it is a hexagon with six sides and a rounded bay entrance.

In 1814, during the War of 1812, the British invaded Washington, D.C., and burned the White House. President James Madison and his wife, Dolley Madison, moved into Octagon House, where they stayed until 1815. The Treaty of Ghent, which ended the War of 1812, was signed on the second floor of Octagon House.

In 1902, the American Institute of Architects bought the Octagon House for its offices. Today, however, it is an historic museum owned by the American Architectural Foundation. Designated a National Historic Landmark in 1960.

**UNITED STATES CAPITOL** The seat of Congress, the legislative branch of the United States. Pierre L'Enfant, the French-born American architect who had laid out the city of Washington, D.C., selected the site of the Capitol. The building's design, however, was chosen through a competition. Seventeen proposals were submitted, but government officials deemed none satisfactory. After the contest had closed, Dr. William Thornton, a physician living in the British West Indies, submitted a plan that the government, including George Washington, approved.

HISTORY Thornton's plans called for a grand building made up of three main sections—a center section topped by a low dome and two wings, one for each branch of Congress. Work began in 1793, and Washington laid the cornerstone on September 18 of that year. Construction was slow and difficult. In 1800, Congress, the Supreme Court, and the Library of Congress moved into the still unfinished north wing.

In 1803, work resumed under the direction of architect Benjamin Latrobe. By 1807, the House of Representatives was able to move into the south wing. The War of 1812 caused work to stop, and in 1814, the British, who had invaded Washington, D.C., set fire to the Capitol.

A sudden storm helped put out the fire and prevented total destruction of the building.

Latrobe began to rebuild the Capitol in 1815, and work continued under his successor, Charles Bulfinch. Improvements were made throughout the 1800s, including the expansion of the Capitol, the replacement of the original low dome with today's impressive dome, and the addition of modern conveniences such as electricity and indoor plumbing. In 1863, the statue of Freedom, weighing 14,985 pounds (6,797 kilograms), was placed atop the dome.

Renovations and modernization continued throughout the 1800s and 1900s. In the 1950s, air conditioning was installed, and the east front was remodeled. Broadcast studios were added in 1979 to allow television coverage of House debates, and in 1986, the Senate also permitted live coverage. Work began in 1983 to structurally strengthen and renovate the west front.

TODAY Beginning in 2000, a new Capitol Visitor Center was planned to be built underground, beneath the east front of the Capitol. This new center, to be completed in 2005, will allow the public to enjoy the Capitol, while maintaining its historical integrity. Designated a National Historic Landmark in 1960.

**UNITED STATES SUPREME COURT BUILDING** The Greek Corinthian-style building in which the highest court of the judicial branch of government, the Supreme Court, has met since 1935. During the first 145 years of its existence, the Supreme Court did not meet in a permanent site. It met in about a

The Capitol's impressive dome is made of 8,909,200 pounds (4,041.2 tonnes) of cast iron. Because the Capitol has been renovated many times, it is impossible to calculate a meaningful cost of its construction.

dozen different places, including the old Senate chamber on the first floor of the Capitol.

HISTORY Around 1912, near the end of his term, President William Howard Taft proposed the idea of a permanent building for the Supreme Court. After Taft became Chief Justice of the United States in 1921, he stepped up his efforts. Finally, in 1929, Congress approved $9.7 million for the project. Although Taft approved the plans for the building, he died in 1930 before construction began.

Different types of marble were used throughout the four-story high building. White Vermont marble was used on the outside. In front of the Court are two large statues created by sculptor James Earle Fraser. The female figure represents justice, and the male figure represents the guardian of law. Over the entrance to the Court is carved the motto "Equal Justice Under Law."

TODAY The main courtroom, the judges' offices, several conference rooms, and exhibit halls are on the ground floor. There are offices for a staff of plumbers, electricians, air-conditioning and heating specialists, and groundskeepers in the basement. The second floor includes the justices' library and dining room and the law clerks' offices. The top floor houses a gym and a storage area. The Supreme Court is open to the public Mondays through Fridays, but visitors are only permitted on the ground floor and part of the first floor. Designated a National Historic Landmark in 1987.

WHITE HOUSE The home of every United States president except George Washington and the oldest government building in the nation. The White House has been remodeled, restored, and redecorated many times during its more than 200-year history.

HISTORY Although Washington never lived in the White House, he helped plan the mansion and chose its site. A self-taught Irish builder, James Hoban, originally designed the house as a three-story Georgian-style home. To save on the cost, Washington told Hoban to eliminate the third floor. (A third floor was finally added in 1927.) The initial cost of the White House was about $240,000.

In 1800, John and Abigail Adams became the first people to occupy the still unfinished home. Only six rooms were usable. Firewood for heating and cooking was scarce, there were no indoor bathrooms, and water had to be carried to the house from a park about five blocks away. Abigail Adams hung the family laundry in the East Room.

Dolley Madison, wife of President James Madison, redecorated the White House but saw it destroyed by the British during the War of 1812. A fire gutted the interior of the house, but the exterior remained, blackened by the smoke. James Hoban supervised the rebuilding wired for electricity in 1891. During President Theodore Roosevelt's terms, the White House was remodeled and expanded. New floors, modern heating and plumbing, and safer wiring were installed. Theodore Roosevelt also issued the executive order changing the official name of the president's house from "Executive Mansion" to "The White House," although it had often been informally called by that name.

In 1948, engineers warned that the White House was structurally unsafe. As in 1814, the interior was gutted and only the exterior walls remained. New foundations, two new basements, air-conditioning, and fireproofing were added. The interior details of the historic home were faithfully recreated. In 1952, President Truman conducted a televised tour of the rebuilt White House.

In the early 1960s, Jacqueline Kennedy, wife of President John F. Kennedy, redecorated the White House and again hosted a televised tour of the beautified home. Further improvements were made during the Nixon and Reagan administrations.

TODAY The White House currently has four floors. The ground floor includes the Oval Office, staff offices, pressrooms, the library, and other historic rooms. The first floor, which opens onto the North Portico facing Pennsylvania Avenue, includes five staterooms that are used for official entertaining. The family's private quarters are on the second floor, along with several historic rooms such as the Lincoln

The White House Historical Association is responsible for maintaining the White House's furnishings, antiques, and paintings, as well as the lawns, trees, and flowerbeds.

of the White House, which was completed in 1817.

Throughout the 1800s, the White House was modernized. Running water was brought to the house in 1833, and a cooking stove replaced cooking over an open fireplace in 1850. The house was

Bedroom. The top floor has extra rooms for the family, guest rooms, and storage areas. Designated a National Historic Landmark in 1960.

## MORE SITES

### FRANCES PERKINS HOME

The Georgian Revival brick townhouse of the first female cabinet secretary, Frances Perkins. She served as secretary of labor in Franklin D. Roosevelt's administration and lived here from 1937 until 1940. Designated a National Historic Landmark in 1991.

### GALLAUDET COLLEGE HISTORIC DISTRICT

Founded in 1864 by Abraham Lincoln, the only center of higher learning specifically for the hearing impaired. Frederick Clarke Withers designed the High Victorian Gothic-style buildings of the campus. Frederick Law Olmsted and Calvert Vaux, two of the most famous landscape designers of the time, planned the gardens. Designated a National Historic Landmark in 1965.

## ★ PROFILE ★
## FRANCES PERKINS

The first female cabinet secretary, who served as Franklin D. Roosevelt's secretary of labor from 1933 to 1945—longer than any other cabinet member.

Perkins was born in Massachusetts in 1882 and graduated from Columbia University in 1910 with a master's degree in sociology. She became involved in New York State government and served under Governors Al Smith and Franklin D. Roosevelt.

Coming to her post in 1933 at the height of the Great Depression, she worked tirelessly to help the common people. Having helped the president write many laws, her efforts resulted in the passage of the Social Security Act of 1935. This law provided—then and now—payments to the unemployed, to disabled workers, and to retired workers. Perkins also worked for the Fair Labor Standards Act, a law that established a minimum wage.

After resigning from the cabinet in 1945, Perkins served as a civil service commissioner until 1952. She then taught and lectured until her death in 1965.

### GEORGETOWN HISTORIC DISTRICT

Originally part of a Maryland tobacco port founded in 1751, but part of Washington, D.C., since 1800. An upscale residential area with many narrow streets, Georgetown includes many well-preserved nineteenth-century buildings. Designated a National Historic Landmark in 1967.

Use this index of historic places to quickly locate the state in which a landmark can be found and the page on which it is described.

| Site or Landmark | State | Page # |
|---|---|---|
| Acoma Pueblo | New Mexico | 70 |
| Adams-Fairview Bonanza Farm | North Dakota | 78 |
| Alamo, The | Texas | 98–100 |
| Albert Einstein House | New Jersey | 67–68 |
| Alvin Cullom York Farm | Tennessee | 94 |
| Amana Colonies | Iowa | 36 |
| American Flag-Raising Site | Alaska | 8 |
| Andersonville National Historic Site | Georgia | 24–25 |
| Anvil Creek Gold Discovery Site | Alaska | 7 |
| Apollo Mission Control Center | Texas | 97 |
| Apollo Theater | New York | 70–71 |
| Appomattox Court House National Historic Park | Virginia | 104–105 |
| Astor Fur Warehouse | Wisconsin | 114 |
| Bannack Historic District | Montana | 61 |
| Bath House Row | Arkansas | 12 |
| Bellevue Avenue Historic District, Newport | Rhode Island | 89 |
| Biltmore Estate | North Carolina | 75–76 |
| Bingham Canyon Open Pit Copper Mine | Utah | 102 |
| Boston Common | Massachusetts | 48 |
| Brooklyn Bridge | New York | 71–72 |
| Cabildo, The | Louisiana | 44 |
| Cahokia Mounds | Illinois | 31–32 |
| Calvin Coolidge Homestead District | Vermont | 104 |
| Cape Canaveral Air Force Station | Florida | 22–23 |
| Cape Hatteras Light Station | North Carolina | 76 |
| Carry A. Nation House | Kansas | 40 |
| Cataldo Mission | Idaho | 29–30 |
| Charles A. Lindbergh, Sr., House | Minnesota | 55–56 |
| Charles M. Russell House | Montana | 61 |
| Charleston Historic District | South Carolina | 92 |
| Cherokee National Capitol | Oklahoma | 80–81 |
| Chicago Avenue Water Tower and Pumping Station | Illinois | 33–34 |
| Chinook Point | Washington | 110 |
| Chrysler Building | New York | 72–73 |
| Churchill Downs | Kentucky | 42 |
| City of Rocks State Park | Idaho | 30 |
| Clara Barton House | Maryland | 48 |
| Cleveland Arcade | Ohio | 78 |
| Colonial Annapolis Historic District | Maryland | 46–47 |
| Cook Landing Site | Hawaii | 29 |
| Council Grove Historic District | Kansas | 40 |
| Cowpens National Battlefield | South Carolina | 92 |
| Crow Creek Site | South Dakota | 94 |
| Danger Cave | Utah | 102 |
| Daniel Webster Family Home | New Hampshire | 66 |
| Deadwood Historic District | South Dakota | 92–93 |
| Dealey Plaza Historic District | Texas | 100 |
| Delta Queen | Louisiana | 42–43 |
| Dexter Avenue King Memorial Baptist Church | Alabama | 5–6 |
| Donner Camp | California | 15–16 |
| Durango-Silverton Narrow Gauge Railroad | Colorado | 17–18 |
| Edison National Historic Site | New Jersey | 69 |
| Eleutherian Mills | Delaware | 21 |
| Elkins Coal and Coke Company Historic District | West Virginia | 112 |
| Emma C. Berry | Connecticut | 18–19 |
| Erie Canal | New York | 74 |
| Ernest Hemingway House | Florida | 23 |
| Eugene V. Debs Home | Indiana | 36 |
| F. Scott Fitzgerald House | Minnesota | 55 |
| Father Flanagan's Boys' Home | Nebraska | 61–62 |
| First Bank of the United States | Pennsylvania | 85–86 |
| Flying Horse Carousel | Rhode Island | 89 |
| Fort Astoria Site | Oregon | 83 |
| Fort Christina | Delaware | 20–21 |
| Fort Churchill | Nevada | 65 |
| Fort Hall | Idaho | 30 |
| Fort Laramie | Wyoming | 116 |
| Fort Leavenworth | Kansas | 39–40 |
| Fort McHenry | Maryland | 47–48 |
| Fort Morgan | Alabama | 7 |
| Fort Sam Houston | Texas | 100 |
| Fort Sill | Oklahoma | 80 |
| Fort Smith | Arkansas | 12 |
| Fort Sumter | South Carolina | 90 |
| Fort Union Trading Post National Historic Site | North Dakota | 77 |
| Fort Walton Mound | Florida | 23 |
| Fox Theatre | Georgia | 26 |
| Frances Perkins Home | Washington, D.C. | 122 |
| Francis G. Newlands Home | Nevada | 65 |
| Frederick C. Robie House | Illinois | 31 |
| French Quarter, The | Louisiana | 43 |
| Gallaudet College Historic District | Washington, D.C. | 122 |
| Gateway Arch | Missouri | 58–59 |
| General Motors Building | Michigan | 53 |
| Georgetown Historic District | Washington, D.C. | 122 |
| Georgia O'Keeffe Home and Studio | New Mexico | 69–70 |
| Gettysburg National Military Park | Pennsylvania | 83–84 |
| Going-to-the-Sun Road | Montana | 59–60 |
| Golden Spike National Historic Site | Utah | 100 |
| Graceland | Tennessee | 95 |
| Grand Canyon Village | Arizona | 9 |
| Grant Park Stadium (Soldier Field) | Illinois | 34 |
| Greenbrier, The | West Virginia | 111–112 |
| Guthrie Historic District | Oklahoma | 81 |
| Hancock Shaker Village | Massachusetts | 52 |
| Harriet Beecher Stowe House | Maine | 44–45 |
| Hearst San Simeon Estate | California | 16 |
| Henry Clay Home | Kentucky | 41–42 |
| Henry Ford Museum and Greenfield Village | Michigan | 54 |
| Herbert Hoover Birthplace | Iowa | 37–38 |
| Hermitage, The | Tennessee | 94–95 |
| Hollenberg Pony Express Station | Kansas | 38–39 |
| Homeplace Plantation House | Louisiana | 43–44 |
| Hoover Dam | Nevada | 63–64 |
| Independence Hall and National Historic Park | Pennsylvania | 87 |
| Indianapolis Motor Speedway | Indiana | 36 |
| Iolani Palace | Hawaii | 27–28 |

| Site or Landmark | State | Page # |
|---|---|---|
| Iron Hill School No. 112 | Delaware | 20 |
| Ivy Green (Helen Keller birthplace) | Alabama | 6–7 |
| Jacksonville Historic District | Oregon | 81–82 |
| Jacobs Hall, Kentucky School for the Deaf | Kentucky | 40–41 |
| James A. Garfield National Historic Site | Ohio | 79 |
| James G. Blaine House | Maine | 46 |
| Johnstown Inclined Railway | Pennsylvania | 87 |
| John Sullivan House | New Hampshire | 66–67 |
| Kahal Kadosh Beth Elohim | South Carolina | 90–91 |
| Kalaupapa Leprosy Settlement | Hawaii | 29 |
| King Ranch | Texas | 97–98 |
| Knife River Indian Villages National Historic Site | North Dakota | 77 |
| Lemhi Pass | Idaho | 30 |
| *Lewis R. French* | Maine | 45 |
| Lexington Green | Massachusetts | 51–52 |
| Liberty Bell | Pennsylvania | 87 |
| Liberty Hall | Kentucky | 42 |
| Library of Congress | Washington, D.C. | 117–118 |
| Lincoln Highway | Iowa | 38 |
| Lincoln Home | Illinois | 33 |
| Little Rock Central High School | Arkansas | 10–12 |
| Little White Schoolhouse | Wisconsin | 113–114 |
| Lombardy Hall | Delaware | 21 |
| Longfellow House | Massachusetts | 52 |
| Lowell Observatory | Arizona | 10 |
| Lucas Gusher Spindletop Oil Field | Texas | 96–97 |
| Mackinac Island | Michigan | 53–54 |
| Madame C.J. Walker Manufacturing Company | Indiana | 34–35 |
| Manzanar War Relocation Center | California | 16 |
| Mark Twain Boyhood Home | Missouri | 57–58 |
| Mark Twain Home | Connecticut | 19 |
| Mayo Clinic Buildings | Minnesota | 54–55 |
| Michigan State Capitol | Michigan | 54 |
| Millford Plantation | South Carolina | 91–92 |
| Milton S. Hershey Mansion | Pennsylvania | 84–85 |
| Missouri Botanical Gardens | Missouri | 59 |
| Monticello | Virginia | 105–106 |
| Mount Independence | Vermont | 103–104 |
| Mount Rushmore National Memorial | South Dakota | 93–94 |
| Mount Vernon | Virginia | 107–108 |
| Mount Washington Hotel | New Hampshire | 65–66 |
| Mountain Iron Mine | Minnesota | 56 |
| Namur Historic District | Wisconsin | 114 |
| Nebraska State Capitol | Nebraska | 63 |
| Nellie Johnstone No. 1 | Oklahoma | 81 |
| New Haven Green Historic District | Connecticut | 19 |
| Niagara Reservation | New York | 74 |
| Octagon House | Washington, D.C. | 118 |
| Ohio Statehouse | Ohio | 79 |
| Old City Hall | Utah | 102 |
| Old Faithful Inn | Wyoming | 115–116 |
| Old North Church | Massachusetts | 48–50 |
| Old Salem Historic District | North Carolina | 76 |
| Old Slater Mill | Rhode Island | 88–89 |
| Old State House (Hartford) | Connecticut | 19–20 |
| Old State House (Newport) | Rhode Island | 88 |
| Oregon Trail Ruts | Wyoming | 115 |
| Owen Lovejoy House | Illinois | 32–33 |
| Parkin Indian Mound | Arkansas | 12 |
| Paul Cuffe Farm | Massachusetts | 52 |
| Pentagon, The | Virginia | 108 |
| Pikes Peak | Colorado | 17 |

| Site or Landmark | State | Page # |
|---|---|---|
| Port Gamble Historic District | Washington | 110 |
| Port Townsend | Washington | 110 |
| Puget Sound Navel Shipyard | Washington | 109–110 |
| Rachel Carson House | Maryland | 48 |
| Rankin Ranch | Montana | 60–61 |
| Robert Frost Homestead | New Hampshire | 66 |
| Robert M. La Follette House | Wisconsin | 114 |
| Rokeby | Vermont | 103 |
| Rosalie | Mississippi | 57 |
| St. Augustine Town Plan Historic District | Florida | 23 |
| St. Michael's Cathedral | Alaska | 8 |
| San Diego Mission Church | California | 13–14 |
| San Francisco Cable Cars | California | 16 |
| Santa Fe Plaza | New Mexico | 70 |
| San Xavier Del Bac Mission | Arizona | 10 |
| Savannah Historic District | Georgia | 26 |
| Shelburne Farms | Vermont | 104 |
| Siege and Battle of Corinth Sites | Mississippi | 57 |
| Skidmore Old Town Historic District | Oregon | 83 |
| Stanton Hall | Mississippi | 56 |
| State Capitol (Atlanta) | Georgia | 25 |
| Stono River Slave Rebellion Site | South Carolina | 91 |
| Susan B. Anthony House | New York | 74 |
| Sutter's Mill | California | 13 |
| Telluride Historic District | Colorado | 18 |
| Temple Square | Utah | 101 |
| Tenement Building at 97 Orchard Street | New York | 73 |
| Tennessee State Capitol | Tennessee | 96 |
| Timberline Lodge | Oregon | 82–83 |
| Tippecanoe Battlefield | Indiana | 35 |
| Tombstone Historic District | Arizona | 9 |
| Trinity Site | New Mexico | 70 |
| Tuskegee Institute | Alabama | 7 |
| Ukrainian Immigrant Dwellings and Churches | North Dakota | 78 |
| United States Capitol | Washington, D.C. | 118–119 |
| United States Supreme Court Building | Washington, D.C. | 119–120 |
| University of Virginia Historic District | Virginia | 106–107 |
| U.S. Immigration Station, Angel Island | California | 14–15 |
| USS *Arizona* Memorial | Hawaii | 28–29 |
| USS *Constitution* | Massachusetts | 50 |
| Valley Forge National Historic Park | Pennsylvania | 86–87 |
| Vassar College Observatory | New York | 73–74 |
| Virginia City Historic District | Nevada | 64–65 |
| Walden Pond | Massachusetts | 50–51 |
| Warm Springs Historic District | Georgia | 26 |
| Washington's Crossing | New Jersey | 68–69 |
| Westminster College Gymnasium | Missouri | 59 |
| West Virginia Independence Hall | West Virginia | 112 |
| Wheeling Suspension Bridge | West Virginia | 111 |
| White House | Washington, D.C. | 120–122 |
| Willa Cather House | Nebraska | 62–63 |
| William Faulkner House | Mississippi | 56–57 |
| William Jennings Bryan House | Nebraska | 63 |
| Williamsburg Historic District | Virginia | 109 |
| Winslow Homer Studio | Maine | 46 |
| Woodbury County Courthouse | Kansas | 38 |
| Wounded Knee Battlefield | South Dakota | 93 |
| Wright Brothers National Memorial | North Carolina | 76 |
| *Wright Flyer III* | Ohio | 79 |
| Wyoming State Capitol | Wyoming | 116 |

# SELECTED BIBLIOGRAPHY

Chambers, S. Allen, Jr. *National Landmarks, America's Treasures*. New York: John Wiley & Sons, Inc., 2000.

Handy, Amy. *American Landmarks: The Lighthouse*. New York: Todtri Productions, Ltd., 1998.

Hendricks, Harmon. *History Preserved: A Guide to New York City Landmarks and Historic Districts*. New York: Simon & Schuster, Inc., 1974.

Huber, Leonard V., and Samuel Wilson. *Landmarks of New Orleans*. New Orleans: Louisiana Landmarks Society, 1984.

Kirk, Ruth. *Washington State National Parks, Historic Sites, Recreation Areas, and Natural Landmarks*. Seattle: University of Washington Press, 1974.

Millard, Bob. *Music City USA: The Country Music Lover's Guide to Nashville and Tennessee*. New York: Harper Perennial Library, 1993.

Miller, Arthur P., Jr., *et al. Pennsylvania Battlefields & Military Landmarks*. Mechanicsburg, PA: Stackpole Books, 2000.

New York City Landmarks Preservation Commission. *Guide to New York City Landmarks*. New York: John Wiley & Sons, Inc., 1998.

Schulze, Franz, and Kevin Harrigton, eds. *Chicago's Famous Buildings: A Photographic Guide to the City's Architectural Landmarks and Other Notable Buildings*. Chicago: University of Chicago Press, 1993.

Sherr, Lynn, and Jurate Kazickas. *Susan B. Anthony Slept Here: A Guide to American Women's Landmarks*. New York: Times Books, 1994.

Speck, Lawrence W. *Landmarks of Texas Architecture*. Austin: University of Texas Press, 1986.

Tinling, Marion. *Women Remembered: A Guide to Landmarks of Women's History in the United States*. Westport, CT: Greenwood Publishing Group, 1986.

## WEB SITES

Chicago Historical Society
www.chipublib.org/004chicago

National Park Service
www.cr.nps.gov/nr/nhl

# INDEX

Page numbers for main entries (including feature box titles) are in **boldface**. Page numbers for illustrations are in *italics*.

Abiquiú, NM, **69**

Acoma Pueblo, **70**

Adams-Fairview Bonanza Farm, **78**

The Alamo, **98–100**, *99*

Albert Einstein House, **67–68**

Alvin Cullom York Farm, **94**

Amana Colonies, **36**, *37*

American Flag-Raising Site, **8**

Andersonville, GA, **25**

   National Historic Site, **24–25**

Annapolis, MD, **46**, *47*

Anvil Creek Gold Discovery Site, **7**

Apollo Mission Control Center, **97**

Apollo Theater, **70–71**

Appomattox, VA, **104**

Appomattox Court House National Historic Park, **104–105**, *105*

Asheville, NC, **75**

Astor Fur Warehouse, **114**

Atlanta, GA, 25, *25*, **26**

Baltimore, MD, **47**

Bannack Historic District, **61**

Bath House Row, **12**

Beaumont, TX, **96**

Bellevue Avenue Historic District, **89**

Biltmore Estate, *75*, **75–76**

Bingham Canyon Open Pit Copper Mine, **102**

Boston, MA, **48**

Boston Common, **48**

Boulder City, NV, **63**

Boys Town, NE, 61, **62**, *62*

Bremerton, WA, **109**

Bretton Woods, NH, **66**

Brigham City, UT, **100**

Brooklyn Bridge, *71*, **71–72**, 111

Brunswick, ME, **44**

The Cabildo, **44**

Cahokia Mounds, **31**, *32*, **32**

California Trail, 30, 38

Calvin Coolidge Homestead District, **104**

Cape Canaveral, FL, **22**

   Air Force Station, *22*, **22–23**

Cape Hatteras Light Station, **76**

Carry A. Nation House, **40**

Casa Blanca Indian Reservation, **70**

Cataldo, ID, **29**

Cataldo Mission, **29–30**

Chang-Diaz, Franklin, 22

Charles A. Lindbergh, Sr., House, **55–56**

Charles M. Russell House, **61**

Charleston, SC, **90**

   Historic District, **92**

Charlottesville, VA, **105**

Cherokee National Capitol, *80*, **80–81**

Chicago, IL, **31**

   Chicago Avenue Water Tower and Pumping Station, **33–34**

Chinook, WA, **110**

Chinook Point, **110**

Chrysler Building, *72*, **72–73**

Churchill Downs, KY, **42**

City of Rocks State Park, *30*, **30**

Clara Barton House, **48**

Clemens, Samuel Langhorne. *See* Twain, Mark

Cleveland, OH, **78**

Cleveland Arcade, **78**, *78*

Collingsville, IL, **32**

Coloma, CA, **13**

Colonial Annapolis Historic District, **46–47**, *47*

Colorado Springs, CO, **17**

Concord, MA, **51**

Cook Landing Site, HI, **29**

Council Grove Historic District, **40**

Cowpens National Battlefield, **92**

Crow Creek Site, **94**

Danger Cave, **102**

Daniel Webster Family Home, **66**

Danville, KY, **41**

Dayton, OH, **79**

Deadwood, SD, **92**

   Historic District, **92–93**, *93*

Dealey Plaza Historic District, **100**

*Delta Queen*, *42*, **42–43**

Detroit, MI, **53**

Dexter Avenue King Memorial Baptist Church, *5*, **5–6**

Donner Camp, **15–16**

Durango, CO, **18**

Durango-Silverton Narrow Gauge Railroad, *17*, **17–18**

Edison National Historic Site, **69**

Eleutherian Mills, **21**

Elkins Coal and Coke Company Historic District, **112**

Ellis Island, 15

*Emma C. Berry*, *18*, **18–19**

Erie Canal, **74**

Ernest Hemingway House, **23**

Eugene V. Debs Home, **36**

F. Scott Fitzgerald House, **55**

Father Flanagan's Boys' Home, **61**

Ferrisburgh, VT, **103**

First Bank of the United States, **85–86**

Flanagan, Father Edward Joseph, 61, **62**

Flying Horse Carousel, **89**

Ford, Henry, 54

Fort Astoria Site, **83**

Fort Christina, *20*, **20–21**

Fort Churchill, **65**

Fort Hall, **30**

Fort Laramie, **116**

Fort Leavenworth, **39–40**

Fort McHenry, **47–48**

Fort Morgan, **7**

Fort Sam Houston, **100**

Fort Sill, **80**

Fort Smith, **12**

Fort Sumter, **90**, *90*

Fort Union Trading Post National Historic Site, **77**

Fort Walton Mound, **23**

Fox Theater, **26**

Frances Perkins Home, **122**

Francis G. Newlands Home, **65**

Franklin, NH, **66**

Frederick C. Robie House, **31**

French Quarter, **43**, *44*

Gallaudet College Historic District, **122**

Gateway Arch, *58*, **58–59**

General Motors Building, **53**

Georgetown Historic District, **122**

Georgia O'Keeffe Home and Studio, **69–70**

Gettysburg, PA, **83**

   National Military Park, **83–84**, *84*

Glacier National Park, **60**

Going-to-the-Sun Road, **59–60**, *60*

Golden Spike National Historic Site, **100**

Graceland, **95**

Grand Canyon, **9**

Grand Canyon Village, **9**

Grant Park Stadium (Soldier Field), **34**

The Greenbrier, *111*, **111–112**

Guernsey, WY, **115**

Guthrie Historic District, **81**

Hancock Shaker Village, **52**

Hannibal, MO, **57**

Hanover, KS, **38**

Harriet Beecher Stowe House, **44–45**

Hatteras, NC, **76**

Hearst, William Randolph, 16

Hearst San Simeon Estate, **16**

Helena, MT, **60**

Henry Clay Home, **41–42**

Henry Ford Museum and Greenfield Village, **54**

Herbert Hoover Birthplace, **37–38**

The Hermitage, **94–95**, *95*

Hershey, PA, **84–85**

Holiday, Billie, **72**

Hollenberg Pony Express Station, **38–39**

Homeplace Plantation House, **43–44**

Honolulu, HI, **27**

Hoover Dam, **63–64**

Houston, Samuel, **99**

Houston, TX, **97**

Independence Hall and National Historic Park, **87**

Indianapolis, IN, **34**

Indianapolis Motor Speedway, **36**

Iolani Palace, *27*, **27–28**

Iron Hill School No. 112, **20**

Ivy Green (Helen Keller birthplace), **6–7**

Jacksonville, OR, **81**

   Historic District, **81–82**

Jacobs Hall, Kentucky School for the Deaf, *40*, **40–41**

James A. Garfield National Historic Site, **79**

James G. Blaine House, **46**

Jamestown, TN, **94**

Jefferson, Thomas, 59, 86, 105–107, **106,** 117, 118

Johnstown Inclined Railway, **87**

John Sullivan House, **66–67**

Kahal Kadosh Beth Elohim, **90–91**

Kalaupapa Leprosy Settlement, **29**

Key, Francis Scott, **47**

King, Martin Luther, Jr., 5–6, *6*

King Ranch, **97–98**

Kingsville, TX, **98**

Knife River Indian Villages National Historic Site, *77*, **77**

Lafayette, IN, **35**

Lawton, OK, **80**

Leavenworth, KS, **39**

Lemhi Pass, **30**

*Lewis R. French*, *45*, **45**

Lexington, KY, **42**

Lexington, MA, **51**

   Lexington Green, **51–52**

Liberty Bell, **87**

Liberty Hall, **42**

Library of Congress, *117*, **117–118**

Liliuokalani, Queen, **27**

Lincoln, Abraham, 33, 45, 113, 122

Lincoln Highway, **38**

Lincoln Home, *33*, **33**

Little Rock, AR, **10**

   Central High School, **10–12**, *11*

Little White Schoolhouse, *113*, **113–114**

Lombardy Hall, **21**

Longfellow House, **52**

Lowell Observatory, **10**

Lower East Side Tenement Museum, **73**

Lucas Gusher Spindletop Oil Field, *96*, **96–97**

Mackinac Island, *53*, **53–54**

Madame C.J. Walker Manufacturing Company, **34–35**

Manzanar War Relocation Center, **16**

Mark Twain Boyhood Home, **57–58**

Mark Twain Home (Hartford, CT), **19**

Mayo Clinic Buildings, **54–55**, *55*

Michigan State Capitol, **54**

Millford Plantation, **91–92**

Milton S. Hershey Mansion, **84–85**

Missouri Botanical Gardens, **59**

Mitchell, Maria, 73–74

Montgomery, AL, **5**

Monticello, **105–106**

Mountain Iron Mine, **56**

Mount Hood, **83**

Mount Independence, **103–104**

Mount Rushmore National Memorial, **93–94**

Mount Vernon, VA, **108**

Mount Vernon Mansion, **107–108**

Mount Washington Hotel, *65*, **65–66**

Mystic Seaport, CT, **19**

Namur Historic District, **114**

Nashville, TN, **95**

Natchez, MS, **56**

Nation, Carry A., **40**

Nebraska State Capitol, **63**

Nellie Johnstone No. 1, **81**

Newark, DE, **20**

New Haven, CT, **19**

New Haven Green Historic District, **19**

New Orleans, LA, 42, **43**

Newport, RI, **88**

New York City, **71**

Niagara Reservation, **74**

Nome, AK, **7**

Octagon House, **118**

Ohio Statehouse, **79**

Old City Hall (Salt Lake City), **102**

Old Faithful Inn, *115*, **115–116**

Old North Church, **48–50**, *49*

Old Salem Historic District (NC), **76**

Old Slater Mill, **88–89**, *89*

Old State House (Hartford, CT), **19–20**

Old State House (Newport, RI), **88**

Oregon Trail, 30, 38, **115**

Orwell, VT, **103**

Owen Lovejoy House, **32–33**

Oxford, MS, **56–57**

Parkin, AR, **12**

Parkin Indian Mound, **12**

Paul Cuffe Farm, **52**

Pawtucket, RI, **88–89**

Pearl Harbor, HI, **28**, 109

Penn, William, **86**

The Pentagon, **108**

Perkins, Frances, **122**

Philadelphia, PA, **86**

Pikes Peak, **17**

Pine Ridge Indian Reservation, **93**

Pinewood, SC, **91**

Pony Express, 38–39, *39*

Port Gamble Historic District, **110**

Port Townsend, WA, **110**

Poughkeepsie, NY, **73–74**

Princeton, IL, **32–33**

Princeton, NJ, **67–68**

Puget Sound Naval Shipyard, *109*, **109–110**

Rachel Carson House, **48**

Rankin, Jeannette, **60**

Rankin Ranch, **60**

Red Cloud, NE, **63**

Revere, Paul, **49**

Ripon, WI, **113**

Robert Frost Homestead, **66**

Robert M. La Follette House, **114**

Rochester, MN, **54**

Rochester, NY, **74**

Rockland Harbor, ME, **46**

Rokeby, *103*, **103**

Roosevelt, Franklin D., 16, 20, 26, 59, 67–68, 122

Rosalie mansion, **57**

St. Augustine, FL, **23**

Town Plan Historic District, 23

St. Louis, MO, **58**

St. Michael's Cathedral, *8*, **8**

St. Paul, MN, **55**

Salt Lake City, UT, **101**, 102

San Antonio, TX, **98**

San Diego, CA, **14**

Mission Church, *13*, **13–14**

San Francisco, CA, **15**

San Francisco Cable Cars, **16**

San Simeon, CA, 16

Santa Anna, Antonio López de, 99

Santa Fe Plaza, **70**

Santa Fe Trail, 40, 70

San Xavier Del Bac Mission, **10**

Savannah Historic District, **26**

Sequoyah, **80**

Serra, Junípero, 13, **14**

Shelburne Farms, **104**

Siege and Battle of Corinth Sites, **57**

Sitka, AK, **8**

Skidmore Old Town Historic District, **83**

Smithsonian Air and Space Museum, 79

Soldier Field (Grant Park Stadium), **34**

Springfield, IL, **33**

Stanton, ND, **77**

Stanton Hall, **56**

State Capitol (Atlanta, GA), *25*, **25**

Stono River Slave Rebellion Site, **91**

Stowe, Harriet Beecher, 44–45, **45**

Sturgeon Bay, WI, **114**

Susan B. Anthony House, **74**

Sutter's Mill, **13**

Taft, William Howard, 120

Tahlequah, OK, **81**

Tecumseh, 35

Telluride Historic District, **18**

Temple Square, *101*, **101**

Tenement Building at 97 Orchard Street, **73**

Tennessee State Capitol, **96**

Timberline Lodge, *82*, **82–83**

Tippecanoe Battlefield, *35*, **35**

Titusville, NJ, **68**

Tombstone, AZ, **9**

Historic District, **9**

Trinity Site, **70**

Truckee, CA, **16**

Tuscumbia, AL, **6**

Tuskegee Institute, **7**

Twain, Mark, 19, 43, 57–58, **58**, 65

Ukrainian Immigrant Dwellings and Churches, OH, **78**

Underground Railroad, 45, 103

United States Capitol, **118–119**, *119*

United States Supreme Court Building, **119–120**

University of Virginia Historic District, **106–107**, *107*

U.S. Immigration Station, Angel Island, **14–15**, *15*

USS *Arizona* Memorial, *28*, **28–29**

USS *Constitution*, *50*, **50**

USS *Missouri*, *109*

Valley Forge, PA, **86**

National Historic Park, **86–87**, *87*

Vanderbilt, George Washington, 75

Vassar College Observatory, *73*, **73–74**

Virginia City, NV, **64**

Virginia City Historic District, *64*, **64–65**

Walden Pond, **50–51**

Warm Springs, GA, **26**

Historic District, **26**

Washington, DC, **117**, 117–122

Washington, George, 46–47, 68, 86, 88, 107–108, 117, 118, 120

Washington's Crossing, **68–69**

Wendover, UT, **102**

West Branch, IA, **37**

Westminster College Gymnasium, **59**

Westport, MA, **52**

West Virginia Independence Hall, **112**

Wheeling, WV, **111**

Wheeling Suspension Bridge, **111**

"White Dove of the Desert," 10

White House, **120–122**, *121*

White Sulphur Springs, WV, **112**

Willa Cather House, **62–63**

William Faulkner House, **56–57**, *57*

William Jennings Bryan House, **63**

Williamsburg Historic District, **109**

Williston, ND, **77**

Wilmington, DE, **21**

Winslow Homer Studio, **46**

Woodbury County Courthouse, **38**

Works Progress Administration (WPA), 82

Wounded Knee Battlefield, **93**

Wright, Frank Lloyd, 31

Wright Brothers, 54, 79

National Memorial, **76**

*Wright Flyer III*, **79**

Wyoming State Capitol, **116**

Yellowstone National Park, **115–116**

Young, Brigham, **101**